SHERMAN HARRIS, JR

WHY YOU WANT TO KNOW ABOUT ME?

SH

Why You Want to Know About Me?

Copyright © 2023 by Sherman Harris, Jr.

All Scripture quotations, unless otherwise indicated are taken from the New International Version.

All rights reserved. No part of this book may be reproduced or transmitted in any form or by any means without written permission from the author.

This book is a memoir. Reflecting the author's present recollections of experiences over time, it has been written after many years. Some names have been omitted, some events have been compressed, and some dialogue has been recreated as accurately as possible from memory.

ISBN 978-0-9884384-6-0 (paperback)
ISBN 978-0-9884384-5-3 (hardback)
ISBN 979-8-3886668-8-8 (Amazon hardback)

Library of Congress Cataloging-in-Publication Data

Cover Design by: Tijania Goodwin, The Divine Connection Agency

Photographs by: Elijah Griffin, Jr., Griffin Vision Media

Published by: Your Ultimate Life Curated Publishing Company

Editor, Amani Jackson

Printed in the United States of America

Dedication

To my wife, Debbie, who managed to have enough faith to see me fail and succeed, and despite very difficult trials, believed in God without wavering.

Table of Contents

Forewords vii

Preface xiv

Part One: Fools and Babes

Words Hurt 2

Altar Boy 4

Preacher Boy 6

Pseudo Friends 8

Mom's Favorite 14

June Bug 20

Dad 34

Don't Be Afraid 39

Protected 43

Daddy 46

Part Two: Life Changes

The Fumble 50

I Quit the Game 52

Over Blessed by Debbie 54

The Basement 61

WHY YOU WANT TO KNOW ABOUT ME?

Humbled 63
Prayer Still Works 66

Part Three: The Turnaround

Passion for Fashion...71
Javiere 74
The Prophet..79
Pop Up Prayer..83
The Favor of God 85
God Is Always Right 88
The Gifts Are Without Repentance 90
Iron Sharpens Iron 93
Bring Jesus Back 96
I Am Not Jesus, But You Can Thank Jesus........97
Growth 99
Pay Attention 102
God Did It...104
The Pandemic 107
In the Flow...109
Jealousy 112
Everything In Moderation 114
Get Rid of Fear and Trust God 116

God Is in Control	120
Blessings On Blessings	125
Driven	127
Worthy	132
Drop the Ball	133
Handle Your Anger	136
God Knows	141
You Are the One	148
If Anyone Asks	154
Acknowledgments	157

WHY YOU WANT TO KNOW ABOUT ME?

Foreword
By Tiesha Berkley

It's been said that we live in a world of denial; we don't know the truth anymore. Many would rather lie because not many people can truly handle the truth. But when the truth is told, it is more precious than time.

Sherman Harris is a man who speaks the truth no matter what. His indomitable authenticity continues to help me see that what one may consider imperfections in themselves is the very thing that sets one apart and makes them who they are. Yet, even with those imperfections, you can still be used and make a powerful impact. Being true to who he is and the things he has spoken over my life has purposed me to let go of my fears, doubts, and the unbelief I've struggled with within myself about my abilities.

He has shown that you don't have to be perfect. You just need to be willing to be used and bold enough to walk in your truth. It's the truth that sets you free; with his truth, he has helped set me free from myself. I see and understand now that your truth is your compass to your purpose.

SHERMAN HARRIS, JR.

Foreword
By Chris Birch

I met Sherman when I was finishing high school in 1993/1994. He and I have been partners or advisors to each other since then. We regularly traveled together on Mondays to Atlantic City to feed his gambling habit. I should also mention that he would call me when I was in Maryland almost every day to play his lottery tickets for him. Many days it was at least $50 a day that he played. We also were involved in a partnership to open a Community Complex that never got off the ground. Sherman lost over $100k, from my memory. I was stuck with outstanding credit cards and later learned to pay them down, but Sherman lost cold hard cash.

We later partnered on a clothing store. We never made much money; we were broken into three times in less than a year, and we walked away the final time they cleaned us out. I started my own business in printing while Sherman took a job at Target. He told me when he got his first check after taxes, Sherman sat down and cried; he had never seen such a small check. After that, we always stayed in contact, but didn't talk much for one year. That's when I saw his brother Lenny's face on the news as missing. I called immediately. For another year or two, we always spoke now and then. But not like before. We reconnected in 2016 when I bought my home and contracted Sherman and his crew to do some upgrades. We just bought a rehab property. Sherman's crew did a wonderful job. As a result, we closed a sale after five days on the market.

WHY YOU WANT TO KNOW ABOUT ME?

Foreword
By Kirk (K.C.) Cross
T.G.B.T.G.

In life, we never know what tomorrow may bring. But what we do know is where the paths and roads we travel on in life can sometimes possibly lead and, at times, ultimately end. *"Why You Want to Know About Me"* is the epic journey and life experiences of a man who came from nothing, that rose through the ranks and against all odds to have something, to almost lose everything, and eventually learn the true meaning of God's salvation and blessings

Some may call it luck, but Sherman knows better. From shooting craps as a teenager on the Southside corners of Alexandria, Virginia, to decades later, owning several flourishing businesses. Sherman "June-Bug" Harris has pretty much run the gamut from A to Z. I grew up watching Sherman evolve from a young man with a sharp street acumen and the natural "gift of gab" years later, becoming one of the most well-known and respected men in the District of Columbia, Maryland, and Virginia (DMV) metropolitan area. He pulled off an uncommon and unprecedented feat on a street level back in the day.

As an outsider, he was embraced, accepted, and allowed to operate several money-making businesses and ventures, both legal and illegal, in Washington, D.C. Such resourcefulness was unheard of during this time. Moreover, his personality and street knowledge allowed him to navigate through the maze of street life and all it entailed.

SHERMAN HARRIS, JR.

Drugs, gambling, women, money, jail, death, and all the other trappings of the life he could withstand and survive. His story is truly one of hope and blessings. It is of God's grace that he is telling his story.

Reading these pages, you will see how Sherman has lived a life that normally only gets told after that person has passed on, usually in backrooms, barber shops, and on street corners or from the walls of confinement. Yet, for unknown reasons, God has chosen for his story to be shared with you, not under those circumstances. We are all blessed by that reality and blessing. Read and enjoy.

To God Be the Glory.

WHY YOU WANT TO KNOW ABOUT ME?

Foreword
By Shivon Kershaw

Often, we proclaim that we want it, but rarely do we offer it. In a world of hurt, apprehension, and uncertainty, the easiest thing to do is withdraw, withhold, and neglect to disclose, all in the name of protecting ourselves. Yet, we need to learn that our failure to be transparent and honest suspends our ability to connect, grow, and overcome. The truth is what sets us free. And despite our habits of hiding behind it, it's when we reveal our vulnerabilities that we can relate to and glean from one another's experiences.

Think of it this way: if we never heard the story of the doubters among those fleeing Egypt or Paul's judgment of early Christians, or the lust in David's eye, or the greed in Judas' heart, there could be generations of people who fall victim to the same obstacles. If the authors of the Bible were too ashamed to share their stories for the sake of their *legacy*, imagine how many of us would have *inherited* the spirit of shame in our disappointments. Yet, our shortcomings serve as stepping stones for our victories. There is power in confessing our sins, repentance of our hearts, and testimonies of triumph, for the Word, says in 2 Corinthians 12:10, "where I am weak, He is strong."

Without question, the enemy desires us to be less than honest, secluded in darkness, hiding in plain sight, attacking our vulnerabilities, and magnifying our faults. John 8:44 characterizes him as the father of lies.

He wants to be the only voice we hear, telling us that our past defines who we are and will always be. But the truth expands our horizons, releases the control of our shackles, and straightens our path forward.

Sherman taught me that. He taught me the value of telling the truth to those around me, especially myself. From him, I learned about the strength of surrendering to God's will and living in Spirit and Truth daily. From our daily talks, I learned that even when honesty did not offer the sweetest of serenades, it was still a beautiful melody, reassuring and comforting to the soul, but the only way Sherman could teach me was by living it first.

Why get to know Sherman Harris? Because he can introduce you to a force greater than armies, stronger than the chains of your past, and more effective than the enemy's tactics. He can introduce you to the truth.

WHY YOU WANT TO KNOW ABOUT ME?

Foreword
By Reverend L. Tremayne Lacey

In life, it is very rare to meet someone who will shoot straight from the hip and tell you what they think, as Sherman does. But truth be told, it is such a rarity that when you encounter a person like that, you want to cherish them. *"Why You Want to Know About Me"* is a riveting and revelatory masterpiece of writing that gives insight into the life of just that type of rare human being in the personage of Sherman Harris.

This rare gift to the Kingdom of God has helped me to discover that in me lies a part of God that I should embrace and not be afraid to share the truth with the world. Since becoming my friend, we have eaten together, traveled, fellowshipped, and prayed together. There is no question that his story will change the mindset of the generations that read it. As my friend would say, there is none like Him!

Preface

This book is a one-of-a-kind memoir. It is a part of the story of my life. It starts from my adolescence and ends with a glimpse of what lies ahead. This book was written for those seeking an answer to their hidden questions; we all have them, don't we? If you have questioned your identity or the power of redemption, this book will help you understand how the journey is never over until you are with Jesus.

I had to learn more about my gift but first had to come clean and learn my identity. My journey to authenticity was filled with extraordinary people who partnered with me and prayed for me to reach my potential, even when I was unsure of my destiny. I knew my motives had to be right, and fear had to be checked.

"Why You Want to Know About Me?" It is a testament of faith required to do what God says, even when He said to walk away from it all, I did. I was left with no money, but I gained everything I needed. I must admit I am a giving addict. I will never be able to give God enough for all He has done for me. God told me to tell the truth, and I share it here. I will talk about my past, growth, and, most importantly, God's grace.

WHY YOU WANT TO KNOW ABOUT ME?

Part One:

Fools and Babes

SHERMAN HARRIS, JR

Words Hurt

*Words can hurt you. In the larger world,
it frames how people think about you,
and it can hurt in lots of little, subtle ways.*
NATHAN MYHRVOID

I was born with a cleft lip, sometimes called a harelip. I was constantly ridiculed, so I fought my bullies daily and struggled with self-confidence. I was called almost every derogatory name you can imagine.

Because of my reckless behavior, my mother came to Saint Joseph's Catholic School, embarrassed me in front of my friends, and threatened to pull down my underpants. I did not cry because I was careful to see if anyone was laughing at me. The next day I beat up the guy who laughed at me. Naturally, I received another whipping from my mother. My mother transferred me to a public school, Robert E. Lee School, for the 8th grade, where I became even more reckless in trying to fit in with my peers.

I was enrolled in the now historical T.C. Williams High School for 9th-12th grades, where I learned to control my aggression when I learned about my gift in sports, particularly basketball. With sports came the girls, although I believed the girls were only interested in the popular jock, not the young man beneath the helmet or off the basketball court.

To be honest, I did not know him either. I would enter a journey of discovery to reveal my identity, but first, I traveled down a path of lies. A path of pretending to be something I was not. To avoid ridicule and name-calling and to try to fit in, I became drawn to a particular group of teens.

I kept my appearance neat and my breath fresh with Wintergreen Lifesavers and Wrigley's Doublemint gum. My popularity grew over the years as I dressed to impress my peers. I always thought that if I dressed nicely, that would deter people from looking at my lip. As a result, the entire school voted me '*Best Dressed of the Year.*'

During my junior year in high school, I was first introduced to shooting craps in the boy's bathroom directly across from the cafeteria, where there was an entry fee just to come in while games were in progress. During that time, I sold cigarettes and donuts for cash to enhance my wardrobe and distract my peers from my obvious imperfection.

The name-calling ceased, as craps became the gateway to everything—I thought I needed to play a role in maintaining control. Something familiar with the game resonated with me; perhaps it was the sense of community or belonging. Like sports, there was an element of competition in the excitement and thrill of playing craps and, most importantly, winning.

SHERMAN HARRIS, JR

Altar Boy

*I believed for a long time I could do
whatever I wanted if I made
my confessions before Sunday.*
SHERMAN HARRIS, JR.

Growing up as a member of the Roman Catholic Church, my mom ensured our family was active and involved. If we did not go to Mass on Sunday, we could not go out to play on Sunday or Monday. Believe it or not, I served as an altar boy and enjoyed serving alongside my friends Stokes, Jack, and Ricky. Our role was to help the priest during Mass by serving communion. On our assigned Sunday mornings, Ricky and I were coupled to serve together, and Jack and Stokes served together.

The priest looked out, respected us, and never tried anything inappropriate with us. Someone may say, how do you know? Trust me; if something like that happened, we would have known. Unfortunately, the Catholic Church priests and other leaders have faced countless sexual abuse allegations. My heart goes out to the victims of these misconducts.

WHY YOU WANT TO KNOW ABOUT ME?

I truly believed that going to confession and asking for forgiveness meant all wrongdoing was forgiven. Every Wednesday and Saturday, I would rush to confession to ensure I could receive communion on Sunday to avoid judgment. Everyone in the church knew you sinned if you did not take communion. We had a small-knit church with no more than 200 regular attendees. Everybody knew everybody.

I believe many have issues with religion because many go through the motions of attending service and confession, but no real change occurs. The change will only happen for those who are open and willing to accept the change. My life gradually changed, but I did not realize why a change was important until much later.

SHERMAN HARRIS, JR

Preacher Boy

*Between the earth and the sky above,
nothing can match a grandmother's love.*
UNKNOWN

During the summer months between the ages of 7-13, I enjoyed spending time with my grandmother Emma Knicks, in her hometown of Charleston, South Carolina. I remember that my grandmother was always on her knees at night. I asked my mother why my grandmother was always on her knees, and my mother said, "She's praying for us, especially you."

I asked, "Why is she praying for me?"

My mother informed me that my grandmother said I was a preacher boy.

I said to myself, *"preacher boy?"*

She saw something in me as a young child before I knew God. My grandmother's prayers protected me. Her prayers held our family together. After she passed in 1973, everyone started to live their lives independently of one another.

My grandmother's prophecy came to pass.

I am honored to share the Good News of Jesus Christ with others. I share the Gospel, and God speaks through me to offer blessings

WHY YOU WANT TO KNOW ABOUT ME?

through the gift of prophecy. Though I have not seen my mother's side of the family in years, I have maintained contact with my father's side of the family. The central theme is the power of prayer within the family.

My grandmother demonstrated the power of prayer early in my life. She did not spend much time talking about what she was doing—she exemplified a faithful life. She trusted God to deliver His promises for my life and the lives of her family. I am eternally grateful for my grandmother's example of the power of prayer. Those South Carolina summers are treasured forever.

SHERMAN HARRIS, JR

Pseudo Friends

What about your friends?
Will they stand their ground?
Will they let you down?

TLC

Like most teens at T.C. Williams High School in Alexandria, VA, I was influenced by my friends. Once, we were sitting in class, and we all agreed to blow spitballs. The ringleader gave us the countdown with hand gestures 4, 3, 2, 1, and release. Once the countdown ended, I was the only one to release my spitball, and the target was the teacher's head. As I looked around, my friends were concealing their spitballs. I was the one sent home for disrupting the class.

Mr. Williams, my math teacher, warned me against what he called "pseudo-friends." Mr. Williams encouraged me not to allow my peers to influence me easily. I was greatly agitated when they did not follow through on the agreed-upon mischief. Pseudo-friends were fake friends. He always said, "Do not let your pseudo friends get you in trouble, Sherman. You are suspended and sitting at home because you let them talk you into misbehaving, and your friends are at school."

Mr. Williams' words rang in my head as I mapped my response to my friend's denial. On my first day back at school, I was greeted by Mr. Williams.

He asked me, "Did you get smarter?"

I replied, "Yes, I got way smarter, Mr. Williams."

The next time they attempted to engage me in a plot or scheme, I pretended to participate as they proceeded with the misdeeds. I realized I needed a real friend and found it in Ronnie.

Ronnie was younger, but he had more common sense than I did. I wanted to fight a guy cheating us out of our money while we were shooting craps. Ronnie told me we would not get any money if we fought the man. He pointed out that since the guy was cheating us, we should just bet the same way he was. So, it made sense for us to follow his lead. As a result of his strategy, we won $800. That day changed how I gambled, and I gained a lifelong friend in Ronnie—a true friend.

SHERMAN HARRIS, JR

A Father's Example

*My father didn't tell me how to live,
he lived and let me watch him do it.*
CLARENCE B. KELLAND

My father worked hard to provide for our family, and despite only having a fifth-grade education, he went into the U.S. Army for four years. He came out of service to take care of his twelve siblings. My father grew up in Cross Canal in Old Town, Alexandria, a historical area known as a community of African American residents who settled across from the Alexandria canal after the Civil War.

My father enjoyed fishing alone or with his friends. My brother went with him a few times, but I never liked fishing. After my father retired, he went to Third Baptist Church. Every Sunday morning, he walked to church. If it rained, he would have someone drop him off and pick him up. When I was younger, I never questioned why he never came to Mass with us. He never seemed interested in regular church attendance until after he retired.

My father always seemed to have money, and I would learn later that it was due to his work ethic—a trait I inherited from him. During my senior year, our family was contacted by the National Institute of Health for a trial surgery to repair my cleft lip. I chose to go without the surgery since I had two prior surgeries and still

WHY YOU WANT TO KNOW ABOUT ME?

endured most of my youth with cleft lip scars. My lip made me look like my father, Sherman Harris, Sr., and my sister Leada. My lip was a distinctive part of who I was—a part of my identity. Despite subconsciously putting my hand over my mouth when I spoke to women, the decision I made not to have surgery is still one I'm grateful for because it is one of several traits I inherited from my father.

I always thought my father was a little too strict with me. I was a senior in high school and had to be in the house before midnight, and my friends would always tease me about my curfew. The rule in my father's house was simple—anything I asked for, I could get on Friday since it was payday. He was shocked to walk into my room to find my latest winnings, hundreds of dollars sprawled across the entire surface of the bed. His look meant business.

He said, "Get the drugs out of my house right now, or I'll call the police."

I said, "Dad ain't no drugs in this house. This money comes from gambling."

I explained to my dad that the older gentleman had taught me how to gamble. He knew one of the men, so I called him to verify that I was telling the truth. He told my dad I won the money from an out-of-town trip playing Chuck-a-luck. After that, I gambled to earn money between 19-25. I did not start hustling until I turned 25, a long time after I left my father's house.

During this time, it was extremely common for two parents to be in the home. I did not know any other way. Marital vows were taken seriously, and only death would separate a family. I never saw or heard my parents argue. I am sure they did, but they never argued before us. I did hear rumblings from my father when my mother mismanaged the household income, but since an argument requires two people, that will not be counted as one. My mother enjoyed gambling, particularly playing bingo and numbers—maybe too often.

My dad would yell my mother's name, "Eleanor," Three times and say, "You are going to have these children sitting outside on the street."

I asked, "Daddy, where are you going?" He said, "up there to pay the bill."

Dad returned after a little while, just in time to join us at the dinner table, eating, talking, and laughing as if nothing had happened. As I got older, I would reflect on these moments, asking my sister if she remembered the few times Dad would shout. Then, finally, he said what he had to say, and it was over.

It reminded me of the Biblical account in Matthew 21:12-14 when Jesus kicked over the tables in the temple, and right after Jesus turned over the tables, He continued His work of healing. My dad was amazing in his dealings with others. He worked for the gas company for 45 years and never missed a day; even though he never drove a car, he would always have someone drive him to work. I do not recall him being sick until he turned 76. He fought for six years before he passed away at the age of 82.

I can count on one hand the number of times I have had a cold. Just like my father, I hardly fall sick. When I do, I wonder what will happen to me. Whatever happens, I know my family will be there for me. Family is the fabric of my life. My father taught me the importance of family.

Several paternal aunts lived long, productive lives before transitioning over the past few years. One lived to see 94 years old, and my surviving paternal aunt is in her mid-80s, and she is something else—she thinks she is in her 60s. On the other hand, I

WHY YOU WANT TO KNOW ABOUT ME?

am still close to my siblings. On my father's deathbed, he encouraged us to remain close, so we decided to get together every third Sunday to fellowship at one another's homes.

It is important to do whatever you can to care for your family. As you continue to read this book, you will read about the hustling and what I did to make money. God delivered me from that lifestyle, but one thing remained throughout my life; I take care of my family no matter what. When they call me, I will do what I can to support them. My father showed me how to provide for my family.

SHERMAN HARRIS, JR

Mom's Favorite

*Moms are the people who know us
the best and love us the most.*
UNKNOWN

My mom was everything to me. She was born and raised in Harlem, New York, and spoke multiple languages. She traveled from state to state as a dancer and a singer; I guess her voice caught my dad's attention during one of her variety show performances in Alexandria. My dad said my mom was a fast talker. He did not realize she was nine years younger until they were married. Eleanor Ford married Sherman Harris, Sr. Together; they had six kids—Sandra, me, Leada, Lenny, Nancy, and Harold.

Sandra is the oldest and is now the matriarch of the family. She is active in her church, enjoys singing in several choirs, organizes trips for the seniors in her church, and enjoys shopping. She is the family's social butterfly and encourages us to continue our monthly sibling socials.

Leada has a quiet spirit; she also serves as a greeter at her church and enjoys shopping and playing Pokeno with Sandra and their social group.

WHY YOU WANT TO KNOW ABOUT ME?

Lenny and I were very close. He was an entrepreneur, loved fashion, and had an eclectic sense of style. When he stepped out, he stepped out in style. He attended church regularly and was well-known for serving as the eyes, ears, and voice for community members who had no voice. He was an ally of the local government of Alexandria. As brothers, we were confidants and shared many of the same interests. He was the ultimate doer.

Nancy is a no-nonsense person and speaks whatever is on her mind. She enjoys cooking; her specialty is our dad's fried chicken. She also enjoys knitting.

Harold enjoys cooking and catering for family and friends' events. He is respected throughout the community as an event planner. He goes out of his way to help others. He loves tennis and is a private tennis instructor. Harold also serves as a mentor to many people in recovery. He works in the mental health field and attends church regularly.

When I was younger, I had a paper route, and my mom went with me every morning at 4:00 a.m. She never missed any of my games when I played basketball and football. She was very involved with all our extra-curricular activities.

Although she was mostly a stay-at-home mom, she was a hustler and would work odd jobs to help my father provide for the family household, including working for the directory for priests. My mother was the glue to keep the immediate and extended family together. She planned all our family gatherings and fish fries.

My mother was something else. She loved and disciplined her older kids the same. The younger siblings caught a break from our mother's discipline. No one was excluded from going to Mass each week. I was probably my mother's favorite child when I think about it. When I'd come home from practice, she would run my shower during my high school days.

I would tell her, "Mom, I just took a shower after practice."

She would say, "Boy, get in that water!"

During my high school years and beyond, I had a lot of different young ladies in and out of my life, but my mom would always take up for me. So often, the young ladies would try to get in good with my mom.

She would tell them, "Y'all cannot keep popping up in my house. I do not know who he is going to bring over here. I don't want any incidents. I would rather for y'all to call me before y'all come. You can come to visit me, but y'all know how he is."

My mom knew how I was, and so did the young ladies.

My mom was a great cook, and she fed everybody on the block except for Fridays because we were Catholics; we normally had fish on Fridays. Sundays were set aside for family. Everyone was welcome to eat at our house Monday through Thursday and Saturday.

My parents ensured we ate together as a family. We did not have this individual thing we see these days where everyone eats at different times and in different rooms. We had chores and were responsible for keeping our rooms clean. The family was important.

My mom sent us to Catholic school during my early years so we could get a good education. After that, she worked hard to contribute to the household by cleaning and caring for the children of wealthy Caucasians. Then, as we got older, she worked for the school system.

My mom was jovial, enjoyed playing cards, and loved her family and community. My mom was a stout, stylish lady and full of life until she became ill and lost a lot of weight. Her stomach pain was misdiagnosed, and after seeking a second opinion, she was diagnosed with rare cancer. Unfortunately, when they found out the cancer had spread throughout her body, it was too late for treatment. Nevertheless, our mom's legacy provided proper instruction, and her discipline positively impacted her children. Her home was a safe place and a haven for a hot meal. She made her presence known and felt not only by our family but also by the community.

SHERMAN HARRIS, JR

The Watch Out

*Birds of a feather flock together
so beware of the company you keep.
Life has no rules that dictate that you
have to be good friends with everyone-
just respectful of them.
You will either become like the persons
you are closest to or
they will become more like you.*
CALVERT JONES

One day, some of my buddies decided they wanted to acquire goods illegally. So, we rode to a local store where my role was the watch-out guy. Well, we got caught. Somehow, the employees knew that I was the watch-out guy. The police arrived, and we were all taken to the police station.

I was held until my parents came to get me. The police warned me not to get into any more trouble. When I got home, I received the "watch out" whipping. I can still feel the whipping to this day. I laugh about it, but I know that whipping saved me. God was always watching out for me.

I still hung out with my buddies but never got in the car with them. Some of them continued to get in trouble and ended up in jail. Sometimes, I look back at my dealings with my friends and realize

WHY YOU WANT TO KNOW ABOUT ME?

the whippings saved me. At that time, I thought my parents were too strict with me, but I see how they watched out to bless and protect me from wrongdoings.

SHERMAN HARRIS, JR

June Bug

I never intended to become the boss.

SHERMAN HARRIS, JR.

Entrepreneurship has always appealed to me. Today's society calls it the 'gig' economy, but small, odd jobs around the neighborhood were nothing new to June Bug. That's what my family called me. Some local, older men, considered powerful or hustlers, inspired me. Seeing their fabrics and outfits made me want to imitate their style.

Drinking, smoking, and getting high never impressed me, so I was fortunate to avoid that lifestyle. I recall visiting my grandfather's favorite hangout, *Down in the Berg,* where drinking guaranteed a loss of self-control.

Even as a pre-teen, I recognized the difference in behavior between an intoxicated person and someone sober. I knew enough to decide I did not want that for myself. Maybe my love for sports outweighed the need to fit in with others who were smoking and drinking. I honestly do not know. To this day, I never smoked a cigarette. I put an unlit cigar in my mouth a few times while hanging out with the guys, but that was the limit.

WHY YOU WANT TO KNOW ABOUT ME?

I did, however, enjoy receiving money from bar patrons. On each visit, I averaged twenty dollars: a lot of money for a kid back then. I quickly became accustomed to having money and developed a certain level of confidence at an early age. I continued to find creative ways to make money throughout my teens. I cleaned barber sinks and shined gentleman's shoes, averaging about a hundred dollars in cash daily.

I visited several colleges offering athletic scholarships, including the University of Southern California and the Universities of North and South Carolina. My high school sponsored my visit to the University of Kansas City. A busload of us went on a weekend trip for that tour, and I thought it was the college I would attend. The girls on the bus started calling me K.C. (my wife's cousin Regina still calls me K.C. to this day).

When I returned from the campus tours, two older gentlemen took me under their wings and taught me how to gamble. Once I started making money, I stopped thinking about college. I decided not to pursue higher education because I began making significant cash. My only regret in this is not pursuing my dream of being a lawyer. I did, however, follow through with my love for coaching.

To make a difference in my community, I coached kids in partnership with the recreation department. I loved coaching young people. I loved coaching sports. I led three undefeated championship basketball teams from 1976 to 1982.

My team won 288 games, losing only 4. I doubt anyone beats that record. Aaron Banks, known by everyone as "PeeWee," was my assistant coach for over ten years. He decided to take advantage of the opportunity to become the head coach of my brother Lenny's team to compete with me in an overtime game in 1982.

In a jam-packed gym, we entered an overtime game. I remember it like yesterday because my best player, Toast, was on the line. I loved to talk trash, so when Toast was on the line, I said, "This game is over." Toast missed his free throw, and the other team rebounded, scoring to win the game. I have not coached a game since. I walked away from coaching, but my heart didn't.

Let me tell you something; on the nights my teams played, no crime occurred. Instead, the newspaper headlines read, "Sherman 'June Bug' Harris is the greatest of all time." The article continued, "If Muhammad Ali came to town, he would have to play second if he came here."

I would ask the people, "Who is the greatest?" They would say, "You are." I loved to talk trash with people. The gymnasium stayed packed on the days my teams played. On one occasion, the mayor asked me if I would coach on a Saturday. I informed him I did not coach on weekends, only during weekdays. The people will come for good talent. Unbeknownst to them; I was unavailable because the weekends were my hustling days.

I loved each of the many years I coached. I attended a game at T.C. Williams High School in 1977: The undefeated Titans. I descended the bleachers to get closer to the action. Then they were down by five points with one minute and 43 seconds remaining in the game. I approached the sideline, and the security officer headed toward me. The head coach told the police to leave me alone. One by one, each player flocked toward the sideline. I told them what to do and returned to my seat in the bleachers. They ended up winning by four points.

The next day, the headline in the local newspaper read, "Who is he?"

WHY YOU WANT TO KNOW ABOUT ME?

I told the team we would be undefeated that year. We couldn't lose this game. "Let's go to work," I ordered.

The point guard was short in stature and quick. Pops, Frank, and Roach were the top scorers. Whenever they saw me, they said, "You are the greatest." They were a talented group of teenagers. I knew they would be a successful team when everyone arrived on time at 6 a.m. Saturday practices.

They asked me, "Why are you laughing, Coach?"

I told them, "Y'all just made yourself undefeated this year."

I told the team that day they had something special anytime you get everyone together, up, and ready by 6 a.m. on a Saturday to come to practice.

Eventually, I became one of the most prominent number writers in Alexandria. Everyone thought I was the runner, but no one knew I was the main man. The booker. The boss. I never showed that I was the big man. Everyone thought the older guy who taught me about numbers was the boss. I never intended to become the boss.

I got into running numbers when a friend writing for someone mismanaged the money and asked me for a loan to settle his debt. I gave him the money. The following month, he came to me for another bailout. I credit him for teaching me everything I know about the game.

A light bulb went off in my head.

I said, "Man, I might as well start as a booker. I am booking it anyway. Let's go get some writers and start booking the numbers."

And that's just what we did. I was booking it anyway. Running numbers is illegal. Instead of going to a convenience store to fill out the lottery ticket, writers met gamblers in barber shops, homes, or any number of agreed locations to pick up the numbers. There were no websites like we have today.

SHERMAN HARRIS, JR

The people who took down your numbers were called number writers. Writers were usually trustworthy individuals in the community. I was the booker. Bookers received the numbers along with the money. When someone hit a lottery number, I paid out the winnings. When someone missed, I kept the money to pay out future winners. Bookers make money when people miss the numbers.

Winning at gambling is not easy. The odds of hitting winning numbers are low. You may have heard about the triple fours a couple of years ago. A television program came out with triple fours as the winning numbers. Everyone across the nation played the numbers; surprisingly, many people won. They broke the bank for the first time in history. Rest assured, there are far more losers than winners in gambling.

Later I played another role. This time the boss, but I acted as a runner. I wanted people to underestimate my financial position. I was okay playing small. Attention shifted from me, and I was okay with it.

Even when I hustled, only a few people knew I was the mastermind behind the operation. People in the street had suspicions, but whenever they saw me, I was busy working as a coach for the youth in my community. They never saw anyone bringing me money or anything along those lines. I always tried to make it seem as if there was someone bigger than me, and there was: God. I just did not recognize or acknowledge Him at that time.

In my mind, playing small had benefits. My friends had nice cars and things. I did not need a Cadillac or Mercedes Benz. I drove a Mercury Cougar. I traded the car out every few years for a new one. I stayed well-dressed because I wanted to look good. My jewelry wasn't flashy. I just wore a ring and a watch. I didn't want too much attention. I was making money without killing or being gang

WHY YOU WANT TO KNOW ABOUT ME?

affiliated. I knew that lifestyle would bring prison and, eventually, death. But, by the grace of God, I listened to His voice, and He saved me many times.

I was the booker, but I wanted people to think I was a runner. So, I had people writing for me. A guy played numbers with me every day for ten dollars. One day he came in talking loud, announcing he had some good numbers. He played for $100. My discernment alerted me that he was up to something. This dude never played $100 in his life. I never wrote numbers down because I have a photographic memory. But he insisted I write the numbers down to ensure accuracy. Reluctantly, I did.

Immediately, I excused myself and went to the bathroom. Once in the bathroom, I folded the numbers into a perfect little square. Using the chewing gum from my mouth, I affixed the paper. Lifting the toilet bowl lid, I secured the gum underneath. I had barely opened the door as the police surrounded the house and my car. I knew the guy was up to something. He set me up. Thankfully, there was no evidence of anything illegal transpiring. My reputation for being a great coach saved me.

During my hearing, my lawyers argued, "Your honor, he is in the paper all the time." The lawyer submitted the newspaper articles and stated, "When does he have time to play numbers?"

He continued, "How does he have time to do what you say he is doing? Furthermore, you did not find anything." Ultimately, the judge asked me if I wanted restitution for damages. I said, "No. I want to leave and return to the basketball court to coach my teams." That was the truth.

The following Monday, I moved from Alexandria, Virginia, to Suitland, Maryland. I knew they would be on me, and I could not risk being charged. I did not want to disappoint my teams. People only saw me in town socializing for a while. I coached my teams and got out of dodge. I was still booking numbers and managing a crack house but from a safer distance. Later, I only returned to Alexandria early in the morning to visit my father during his illness.

Back then, I considered myself wise. I had no clue about my gift. One night at a gambling joint, I heard a voice say, "Go." I left. I never questioned the voices. Did I know what was happening? I wasn't familiar with The Spirit, so no. If I did, I probably would have tried to save my buddies. Whenever someone was with me, I would tell them, "If I tell you, let's go, don't question me. Let's go." On one occasion, we left, and 15 minutes later, the place got robbed.

People could have thought I set it up; instead, they came to me and said, "You just missed it. We got robbed after you left." My obedience to the voice earned me the reputation of a gentleman gangster, another role I played during this time.

WHY YOU WANT TO KNOW ABOUT ME?

A Gentleman Gangster

*Outside of my crew,
no one knew I was the
brains behind the operation.*
SHERMAN HARRIS, JR.

After graduating from high school, my love for sports continued to grow. I was a sports fanatic. I was able to continue to pursue my love for sports by coaching. I loved everything about sports. A friend of mine went to jail, and before his sentencing, he reached out to me for help. He asked me to take care of his remaining supply, instructing me to give his lady a portion of the money for each kilogram (key) of cocaine. He told me I was the only one he trusted. I did not know anything about selling drugs, and I was honest with him about it because I had no idea how to manage such a business.

Sensing this, he appealed to my strength and began to talk dollars. I talked to a buddy of mine, and he said we could make a lot of money. But my buddy told me this was a different level than selling weed. When selling drugs, we must be mindful of traffic flow in and out of the house. But, he continued, "If he wants a particular amount, you can make the same amount and even more with each additional key."

He said I could "walk it slow" and make even more. I was adjusting to the terminology and process for distribution. After he provided an additional explanation, his methodology made sense to walk it slow after he warned, "There is going to be traffic." This meant people would show up once the word got out. I was willing to take a chance.

He kept enticing me, "You could make a large profit from this." So, we started breaking it down; sure enough, the rest is history. I settled with the young lady, giving her a share of the proceeds. Once I completed that transaction, I started overseeing my distribution of the remaining supply.

When the rest of the U.S. suffered the Reagan Recession, we sold coke and dressed in the finest fabrics in the area. Still, I managed not to draw attention to myself. Even then, the Lord had His hands on me, protecting me from harm and danger. Before a club was busted or robbed, something would compel me to leave, although many thought I had a heads-up. Those closest to me knew I had a discerning spirit.

    We set up a house in Alexandria with careful oversight by a reliable female. I trusted her management abilities, and everyone respected her. She started with me selling an ounce, noticing that most of the action occurred at night. Together we developed a team of dealers.

She trusted my approach to let the little guys buy from us and sell at night. I recognized the importance of supply and demand. Our system lasted for several years. Dealers would purchase a few ounces from her and sell them. Then, they would come back to her for more. We had the best product money could buy because it was

WHY YOU WANT TO KNOW ABOUT ME?

pure; we did not sell it cut. This allowed them to make money because they would turn around and return the money to us anyway when they returned for more. Outside of my crew, no one knew I was the mastermind behind the operation. They only assumed.

I had no idea of the road ahead, but my hometown was the backdrop of my transformation. God can bless you even when you're doing wrong because of His journey and superior plan for you.

None of the guys got busted, but we were robbed once for an ounce of drugs. We knew who it was, and the guys asked me, "What do you want us to do to him?"

I said, "Nothing."

I went to the thief and said, "Do you know who you just took that from?"

Back then, people were wary of me. I carried myself a certain way. This birthed my alias, Gentleman Gangster. I realized this when I went to the toughest projects in D.C. and saw my control in those areas. It confirmed something extraordinary had taken place in my life. I considered myself lucky, and people took a liking to me. I frequented places many people did not survive. Strangers don't easily nor often invade their territory, especially usurping drug distribution. My operation thrived within the worse housing projects in D.C.

I sold drugs, made a lot of money, walked around with pockets packed full of cash, and no one ever robbed me. As I look back and think about it all, I see God. He took care of me. I did not know anything about His grace, but now I recognize it as such.

Some people credit it to the kind way I treated people. Unfortunately, jealousy rears its ugly head even when you treat people well. You can have all the money you want; it doesn't prevent people from negatively impacting you. God shielded me from that too.

People kept me abreast of what others were saying about me. I heard, "You were a gentleman. You looked out for others and never said 'no' to people." If someone wanted to do something terrible to me, others would handle it for me. In D.C., they called me 'Bug' or 'Money.' If you knew me as June Bug, we go way back. If you knew me as Bug or Money, you were from my D.C. and Maryland periods. I transformed and performed to fit each persona. It took me some time to discover my true identity.

WHY YOU WANT TO KNOW ABOUT ME?

No One Is That Smart

I only took on the persona to get paid.

SHERMAN HARRIS, JR.

I will say this; nobody is smart enough to hustle. There is, however, a mindset about hustling, especially when we can get away with something. Think about it.

I do not know anyone who drives the speed limit every day. If the speed limit is 40 miles per hour and you travel 5 miles per hour, that is still not the limit. We speed every single day. We may not get caught or receive the ticket. I almost got a ticket one year ago. I have been driving for over 40 years and only received one ticket. I got pulled over for speeding. The officer was in the process of writing the ticket but did not issue the ticket, only a warning.

I have only gotten one ticket and one accident. I hit a lady accidentally. I thought I saw her, but then I did not see her. I believe she accelerated, and I hit her. I tried to use psychology with the police officer, but he did not go for it. As soon as I pulled over, I called my lawyer.

The officer ordered me to put the phone down, and I informed the officer that I was not putting the phone down. My lawyer was still on the phone, and I was afraid.

I told the officer, "If you want to shoot me, then shoot me because I will not get off the phone." I told the officer the lawyer's name. The officer said, "I just want to talk to you."

He informed me that the accident was my fault, and I said, "Ok, sir." Yet, I did not get off the phone. My reaction should not be the initial response, but so much is happening around us daily. He could have easily thought my phone was a weapon, and I only thought about all of that after the fact. I must admit, I acted a fool. I was mad at myself for the accident.

I watch what fear and anger do to us. It will cause us to act out of character. It is like a split personality. I have learned not to allow fear, anger, or madness to resort to an inappropriate reaction, especially with law enforcement. I learned that from hustling. That is why I never wanted to be out front.

I wanted the money more than the status and prestige. I did not want to be this out-front guy. I would have been fine if I could get the money without being out front. I thought I had to play that role in ensuring they paid me, as I only took on the persona to get paid. I would have never stepped out there, but I had to ensure they had enough respect to pay me. That is what made this boastful image come out. I was much more comfortable staying in the background if I could get away with it and still get paid.

I now understand this mindset. People will take advantage of you if they think they can. When I think about it, I took advantage of how people respected me. But I knew where to draw the line. So, I just made sure they did not mess with my money.

WHY YOU WANT TO KNOW ABOUT ME?

Sometimes I would go to someone if they owed me money. I told the person that I owed money to someone else due to their delinquency in paying me. Then, I encouraged them to pay me, and they would pay. I learned this strategy from watching others interact in the world and on television.

Television messed me up when I watched the movie "Godfather." The movie opened my eyes to the importance of paying attention to human behavior. For example, if someone came to me to buy an ounce and the next week, they wanted four ounces; I would not sell it to them. I automatically assumed they were informants. So then, not only will I no longer allow you to purchase from me that day, but I will also never sell to them again.

There was a structure to the hustle. The clients came to my lieutenants, and my lieutenants would come to me. I eventually called a meeting to inform them that if anybody came to you to increase their purchase drastically from one ounce, we would not sell to them anymore. If we were going to be in the game, we had to pay attention to human behavior.

SHERMAN HARRIS, JR

Dad

I watch miracles around me every day.
I experience miracles, and they amaze me.
SHERMAN HARRIS, JR.

A promiscuous lifestyle was a normal part of life for me. After high school, I dated a girl during her senior year in high school, and she got pregnant. We spoke to her mother about the options, and she agreed to an abortion because it was important for her to finish school. She agreed when she told me she did not want to continue the pregnancy, and I was happy because I wanted her to graduate.

To support her decision, I took her to have an abortion. Six months later, we broke up when she said I made her get rid of the baby. She did not speak to me until years later. Then, she told me she had forgiven me for everything that had transpired. Her child would have been my first child.

They say never mix business with pleasure, but sometimes lines are crossed. I had a great hustling relationship with a young lady. I was hustling, and she helped sell the product. It was not an intimate relationship; however, one day, she was there, and one thing led to another. There was no true romance because I had a girlfriend at the time, but we had an understanding. She was the main woman, but there were others.

Even during this time, I believe God was working on me. We decided to travel to New York to terminate the pregnancy of our unborn child at four months gestation. We were faced with making a difficult decision. The decision to terminate a pregnancy was not the first time for me, but this time was different. We made it to New York, just three blocks from the abortion clinic, my nerves became unsettled, and something within me gave me pause for concern.

I called and informed my girlfriend I was having a baby with another woman. I informed her of the voice that told me to keep the baby.

She said, "Okay, we will raise the child."

We discontinued the conversation, and I turned to the woman and told her I did not know what it meant, but we were going to keep the baby. I will never forget it. It was weird that my girlfriend was so accepting of a baby by another woman. The mother of my child agreed to continue the pregnancy, and I was blessed to welcome Tamekia into the world. We call her Meka. I continued to hustle to ensure my child had everything she needed, especially family.

My youngest sister, Nancy, helped take care of Meka. She was babysitting when Meka was just 2 months old when her mother dropped her off with my sister and never returned to pick her up. Finally, Nancy filed and officially adopted Meka. After that, I didn't have a relationship with my daughter for a long time because I was busy hustling. My father always told me to take care of my child, regardless of the relationship with her mother. I always said regardless of how much I traveled the streets. I would take care of my responsibilities as a father.

I am grateful to my youngest sister Nancy for raising my daughter. I always thought that by providing money to my family, I was being supportive. While I was blessed to provide money, I realized a relationship required more. Once Meka entered T.C. Williams high school around 16, our relationship improved.

Meka ended up having a good relationship with her biological mother with no animosity. Aside from giving her life, her mother never did anything for Meka, but she wanted to keep her mother's last name. Meka was an academic student in high school, graduated, and enrolled at Virginia Commonwealth University, and she was doing well in college. During her sophomore year, my daughter got pregnant by an older man. I was frustrated with her decision. She said, "I love you, but I must live my life."

I didn't say anything else about her decision to get married, although I think about it all the time since she was so excited about attending college. I debated whether to attend the wedding, but the Spirit said, "Go." So, my sister and I attended the ceremony held at the justice of the peace. They are still married and are doing okay. They now have three children together, own a home, and she is happy.

I am proud of my daughter. She is a very nurturing, loving, and engaged mother. Not only is she a soccer and track mom, but she is also active in her kids' schools and spends quality time with them. Since she is so busy working and caring for her children, she has little downtime, but when she does, she enjoys relaxing outdoors and working puzzles.

I am blessed to have three grandchildren: Alicia, Stephen Jr., and Sebastian, we call him "Flash." Stephen Jr. (we call him Junior) loves playing games, football, and basketball. He was honored to name his youngest brother Flash. We compromised and named him

WHY YOU WANT TO KNOW ABOUT ME?

Sebastian "Flash" because he arrived quickly. One push, and he was out in a flash! Sebastian loves dinosaurs and cars. Stephen recently asked his mother about going to go to church with Granddaddy and wants to get baptized.

My granddaughter Alicia towers over her peers. She is almost six feet tall. She enjoys track and is a soccer record holder in Fairfax County, Virginia. She is an unbelievable athlete and extremely competitive. But she must learn how to lose gracefully. To be truthful, I was a bad loser too. So, we are bringing her up and letting her compete with older kids.

I'm not just bragging because she is my grandchild, she is a very skilled player, but she was not being challenged. Alicia participated in the 220-meter race in the Penn relays in 2021. Her coaches wanted her to run with older kids. She placed second place. She cried all the way home. My daughter called me and asked me to talk with her. As a former coach, it is second nature for me to encourage athletes. I wanted my granddaughter to realize the significance of her feat since she ran against older kids, and she still placed second. I wanted her to know what a great accomplishment she had earned. I had to break that down to her. She is a gifted girl. Like most teenagers, she loves shopping. So as her granddad, I choose to spoil her. I enjoy taking her shopping to get tennis shoes and whatever she wants.

I prayed for a relationship with my daughter, and by the grace of God, we are now close. Closer than we have ever been since she was born. I appreciate the relationship my daughter has with my sister. Sometimes when we are out for dinner, my daughter calls my sister mom, and she calls me dad. Those who do not know our family dynamics give me a confused look. Nancy is as sweet as she can be, but she is no-nonsense and will take the time to explain as only she can.

When my granddaughter calls to check on me, I ask her how she is doing in school. She already has 11 sports scholarships. Alicia is a gifted girl. I agreed to pay to help her be her best. I also understand she will lose some races, but it builds character. It must be a team effort.

Meka's mother passed away a few years ago, and we attended the funeral. Meka remains in close contact with her biological siblings. I always wondered if parents have a favorite child. I wonder because I have not experienced such bias as a parent since I only have my daughter. I am grateful I was obedient to the voice on that day in New York.

Years later, I received notification that I could have fathered another child, but I later learned that the mother had miscarried. I am thankful for the privilege of being Meka's dad. One of my life's greatest gifts is having healthy relationships with my grandchildren.

WHY YOU WANT TO KNOW ABOUT ME?

Don't Be Afraid

*Don't be afraid to tell the truth –
we're programed to lie,
society rewards lies,
but the truth saves.*
SHERMAN HARRIS, JR.

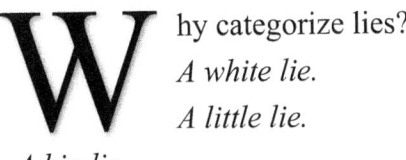

hy categorize lies?
*A white lie.
A little lie.
A big lie.*
Why do we put titles on a lie?
A lie is a lie. I have heard the term white lie many times.

I became accustomed to a lifestyle of deception. I lied about many things to portray myself as someone else. Lying made me feel better about my insecurities and chances for acceptance. To my friends, I looked successful, and everyone liked me because of the image I projected.

Recently, I spoke with someone regarding their upcoming court hearing, and I encouraged him to tell the truth. You think manipulating the truth will keep you from incarceration. I asked him, "Is a lie guaranteed to keep you out of jail?" I advised him to be honest. I believe we are afraid of the opinions of others. Why do you think honesty is hard?

Earlier in life, I was considered a square; someone on the straight and narrow path, often ignored by my peers. This position came with no respect. Since they looked over me, I decided to embellish stories to become significant in their eyes. That reflected my low self-esteem. Hustling wasn't ideal, but I wanted the money and the image. Little did I know God was protecting me during that time. Consider all the lies we tell, thinking they are our salvation.

I lied to the girls. I lied so much; I was the king of lies. A perfect example was when I forgot I told one girl I was in New York. Then I forgot I told another girl I was in Atlanta and another in North Carolina. I had it all twisted.

One day, one of them got me good. She said, "Oh, you will be in Danville?"

Mind you; I was in Danville when she asked me the question. At the time, I was messing around with multiple women in Danville and forgot which one I told to meet me at the hotel. A couple of them showed up in the same room at the same time.

On that day, I said, "This is enough!"

That was a turning point in my life. I knew I could not continue living a life of lies. I began to tell the truth. To my surprise, I attracted more women. The women appreciated my honesty and accepted me for who I was. I met a young lady in a club in North Carolina. I told her we could be friends when I visited, but hopefully, she would not have a jealous boyfriend. This way of talking to ladies worked everywhere I went.

I asked God, "Why would you bring that to my attention for this book? God, what are you trying to show and tell me?

WHY YOU WANT TO KNOW ABOUT ME?

God said, *"Look where you came from. I took you from the streets and protected you. You never went to jail. I kept you out of harm's way. Don't you think I have a plan for your life?"*

I tell people that God can still bless them even when they do wrong. It is His grace and mercy. I believe I had a team of prayer warriors, like my grandmother, family members, and friends. I've always felt that.

I thought I needed several women to prevent me from getting hurt. I saw many brothers get heartbroken by women and figured it would soften any blows if I had multiple. If one left, I would have a few others. That was not true. One of my women left, and I fell apart. I was moaning and groaning, even having the other women. But as a man, I wanted the one that did not want me. I did have some feelings for the one who left me. After I could not get her back, I thought, "Wow, I am not as irresistible as I thought."

The remaining women could not make up for the one. My fear of abandonment forced me to learn different ways of handling my relationships. I hoped if I cared enough for a woman, she would not leave. Still, the women could not satisfy me since the root issue was that I did not feel good about myself.

This will be news to anyone who knows me. I went to a psychiatrist from 1989-1991. God asked me to release this. It is okay to seek help if you feel you need it. The sessions helped me identify some of the sources of my problems. We examined intimate details of my life. She disclosed that as I shared, she became comfortable sharing the issues she was experiencing with her husband. I shared some things with her to remind her she was still young and growing in her relationship with her spouse. She developed feelings for me, creating an ethical dilemma, so she offered to transfer me to another therapist.

In life, you must be truthful to yourself. I remained wise enough to know the importance of telling the truth versus lying. No matter how much I was in the street, I knew I would be okay if I told the truth. I lied so much to appear to be hip to other people. I lied so much and got away with it; I thought it was acceptable. The most dangerous thing you do is think you're getting away with a lie. Don't be afraid to tell the truth.

WHY YOU WANT TO KNOW ABOUT ME?

Protected

I feel like I am spoiled by God.

Sherman Harris, Jr.

I always had a contact who delivered my supply, but one day, our supply ran low, and I had to travel to New York to meet the connection. Our plan was for me to only travel with the product. If anyone got busted, I was responsible for getting them out of jail, and I would no longer maintain contact.

I had my main woman at the time, who led the way for a transaction. We trailed her in another vehicle. The police stopped her, so we made a U-turn to check on her. When we returned, she was already gone. We got off at the next exit, pulled over, and she pulled up beside us, laughing hysterically. She said, "I showed my license, and he let me go." After that day, I began to look at her differently. I later learned my main woman was using drugs.

God protected me even when I was doing wrong. Acts 10:34-35, Peter explained that God is no respecter of persons. I know this to be true because I am one of God's non-respected people. God knows everything. He does not show favoritism; however, I feel spoiled. (Romans 2:11).

I used to ask God all the time, "Why would you do this for me?" God reminded me, "why not you?"

I stopped asking when God told me I did not have to be a great speller or speaker to do God's will. There is no reading or intelligence required to be obedient.

The Bible tells us His ways are not our ways. Do not always think that things just happen. If you see something out of the ordinary, pay attention. When we see, hear, or experience things out of the ordinary, we think it harms us, but it may very well be to protect us.

My wife heard a noise in the house; it sounded like it was in the basement; during this time, our neighbor discovered that someone was trying to break into her house. I told Debbie that the noise may have deterred the burglars from robbing us. The noise kept them away because they thought someone was in the house. As a result, I believe that we were protected.

We found out later the noise was coming from the attic. God protected us. If God allows you to see something, do not take it lightly. Little things can be God speaking or showing us something.

Meditate on this scripture:

> *"For my thoughts are not your thoughts, neither are your ways my ways," declares the* LORD. *As the heavens are higher than the earth, so are my ways higher than your ways and my thoughts than your thoughts."* Isaiah 55:8-9 (NIV)

I was an owner of a nightclub and wore a big, brimmed hat, dressed to the nines in my long trench coat. One night we left the club on our way to Atlantic City. The police pulled over my boys and me. At that time, I had a large quantity of money on me. The police requested my guys to exit the vehicle, where they were searched and roughed up. The police never requested that I get out of the car. It was as if I was not there. I practiced my speech. I thought I would tell them I am a club owner, and I am going to Atlantic City with my buddies to have fun.

During that time, I was foolish, laughing and cracking jokes about how untouchable I was as I watched them being searched and questioned. I always thought I was lucky, but at the time, I did not recognize it was God's favor. The guys in the streets thought I paid the police for protection because I never got busted, but I did not. My boys always protected me, and I wanted to do all I could to protect them. Protecting them meant I would need to take care of any legal issues should the need arise. I always kept a lawyer on retainer.

I realized later that the protection was God. In the same way, God protected me; He protected my guys. He covered all of us. God is the best insurance policy in the world. I thank God for protecting me. I believe God protects fools and babes, and I am both.

SHERMAN HARRIS, JR

Daddy

They did not want that Daddy trouble.

SHERMAN HARRIS, JR.

I managed and was a partner to one of the hottest clubs in Maryland in the 1990s. A part of a famous R&B duo once owned the club. They struggled to keep the club in operation despite a unique concept of a three-story club consisting of a jazz lounge on one level, a club, and an oldies and goodies section. I was informed of the opportunity and saw the potential to make great money.

Everyone from surrounding areas would come to the club by busloads on Friday and Saturday nights. An unfortunate shooting resulted in a death, and the club struggled to rebound. God showed me the opportunity to bring in Go-go bands. Go-go music originated by African American musicians in Washington, D.C. We were the first to start bringing the top bands in the area to clubs in Maryland. Go-go bands saved the club, and attendance increased significantly.

We added oldies but goodies on Wednesday nights, which kept our revenue steady. Next, we started booking rappers to make special guest appearances. Eventually, we added female and male

WHY YOU WANT TO KNOW ABOUT ME?

exotic dancers. The exotic male dancers were downstairs on Tuesday, and the exotic women dancers were upstairs. The exotic female dancers gave me the nickname "Daddy."

One snowy night, I received multiple calls to close the club. The lady who ran the door asked if I would take a chance and open for the night. She said she could get out and drive to the club.

I said, "Yeah, let's open!"

You are not going to believe this. It was one of the best nights ever for the club! The snow was coming down hard, but it did not stop the people from coming to the club. Over three hundred came to see the twenty exotic dancers. The females came out of the woodwork. The club was jammed packed beyond capacity. I figured the professionals and government workers knew they would be off work the next day, so they partied all night into the early morning.

It was a memorable moment to see people willing to come out in the snow to have a good time. To think, I almost closed the club that night. We wanted to renew the lease in 1995, but the city had other plans for the site. Years later, after the club in Maryland closed, I met Big Mike and Donald, the owners of a popular nightclub in Washington, D.C., when they agreed that my exotic dancers from the Maryland club would perform twice a week at their club. They performed so well that they were invited back every night; thus, our partnership and friendship grew, and so did the money.

All the celebrities and rappers would make guest appearances. The D.C. club was the hottest spot. All the headliners of that time would come. Big Mike would receive calls all the time, asking if Daddy could hook them up with dancers.

We also had a few after-hour spots designated as private parties for customers to attend after the club closed at 2 a.m. But, again, we ensured the celebrities remained anonymous.

I encouraged the dancers to be true to themselves. I said, "If you are a dancer, just dance and be the best dancer, you can be."

A lot of the dancers reached out to me to thank me for not allowing them to go down a path not intended for them. I never forced or encouraged anyone to do anything they did not want.

I was once accused of being a pimp, but I politely made it clear that I was strictly the manager. I protected the dancers. I got my percentage; they got theirs. I did not have any personal involvement with them. I did not beat them. There is no way I could be a pimp. I was their manager, plain and simple.

My philosophy was to treat the dancers respectfully, even in the dance world. Although for seven years, I managed 66 female dancers, it was strictly business. I was dating Debbie when I had the club. She was committed to our relationship, and so was I. She trusted me, despite being surrounded by naked dancers every night. She trusted me even while we were engaged.

There was a time when the dancers called me day and night. Some of them went to New York for a party and I did not go with them. One of them tried to contact me because the guy that hosted the party would not pay them. I did not hear my phone ring, so she called Debbie's house at 2:45 a.m.

Debbie informed the dancer that she did not mind her calling but instructed her never to call her home at that hour unless someone died. The girl apologized and explained the situation. That was the first and last time Debbie had that conversation. She set a firm boundary, and it was never crossed again. I told the dancers to say, "I work for Daddy." The money was released immediately. No one wanted any trouble because Daddy did not play. People feared me, and I knew it, but I did not do anything for them to believe otherwise. I let them believe whatever they chose to believe.

WHY YOU WANT TO KNOW ABOUT ME?

Part Two:

Life Changes

SHERMAN HARRIS, JR

The Fumble

*I could not risk my reputation
by getting caught selling drugs.*
SHERMAN HARRIS, JR.

You will not remain the same when the Spirit of God changes you. I am a witness that your life will improve when you study and apply God's word. It is impossible to keep studying God's word and remain the same. When I began hustling, I pretended to be someone I was not. I did not know anything about selling drugs. I maintained a hustler persona for almost 40 years. When I look back, I know God was protecting me. When I began to learn about the Christian life and not just about religion, I learned I could have a relationship with God.

When I was hustling, God cared for my team and me even when I was doing wrong. We had a crack house in the 1980s for three years. The house was making thousands of dollars a week. I oversaw operations at the house, all while coaching.

While in high school, I always played football throughout my junior year. However, I never played organized basketball until my senior year. I was told I would not make the team; however, not only did I make the team, but I was also the sixth man and earned *'Defensive Player of the Year.'*

I coached four teams winning teams. As a result of my winning reputation, I had several offers to coach at schools. I declined the offers because of the life I was living. I did not want my wrongdoings to interfere with my image as a great basketball coach. I was always concerned about my image. Looking back now, I wish I had taken advantage of the opportunity to coach at a school. In my opinion, many high school and college coaches are not naturally gifted.

Coaching was not about the money; it was about the kids. I was fortunate then to realize I did a good job at coaching. I knew how to recognize and promote raw talent. For example, if I saw potential in a player, I knew how to motivate them to perform at their highest and best level. I picked up players other teams cut, and they became All-American Athletes. Not just once, it happened several times. When I coached, between 40-45 athletes came to tryouts. I could only carry 15 players. Everyone wanted to be a part of the team. Not just any team, but the winning team.

God gifted me with the ability to watch sports, identify the key players, and predict the outcome. A buddy of mine confessed to making thousands of dollars from our conversations about upcoming games. I figured out what he was doing, and we stopped having those conversations. I have no desire to make money from God's gift. I always thought I was lucky to guess; little did I know it was discernment from God, and later, I possessed the prophetic gift. I did learn that even when I fumbled, God always set me up to recover and gave me another chance.

SHERMAN HARRIS, JR

I Quit the Game

I knew it was time to walk away.

SHERMAN HARRIS, JR.

The year was 1988, and I gave it all up. I gave up hustling. There was dope on the street called O.J. Simpson. This drug wreaked havoc on the lives of many people. One of my friends overdosed. I walked in on my brother, in a vulnerable position, high on cocaine. Thankfully he was admitted into D.C. General Hospital for a thirty-day drug treatment program. Once he was released, he never looked back or used drugs again. This event changed my life forever.

After these events, I never looked back to a life of hustling. I knew it was time to quit the drug game. Within a few days, I gave away my stash and did not ask for any money. I knew it was time to do something else.

I started investing in nightclubs. I also started gambling seven days a week. I enjoyed sports betting and all aspects of gambling. I did not enjoy hustling because I did not want to risk going to jail. The game was too risky, and I no longer wanted to be involved. I knew it was time to walk away when a guy confronted me with a pistol pointed at me. Thank God I walked away unharmed.

When I thought about it, I never knew who I was. I was always role-playing. Plenty was never enough. I always wanted more. I believe it was my ego. I never knew I could have real friends until I got a relationship with God. I have always had associates all my life. I had one friend: Ronnie, and we are still friends to this day.

SHERMAN HARRIS, JR

Over Blessed by Debbie

*I do not want to think
about what my life would be
like without my beautiful wife.*
SHERMAN HARRIS, JR.

When I think about it, I was over-blessed with Debbie. We met in 1971 at T.C. Williams High School during her freshman/sophomore year. After that, we reunited every few years. I called Debbie or received calls from my sister, friends, and other family members to reestablish our relationship. We went to dinner, movies, etc., and dated for a short period. We repeated this cycle until we established a permanent relationship in 2000.

Before my father passed in 1999, he told me that Debbie was the one. My dad told me if I did not get married before I was 50, I would never get married. I would remain a bachelor. Being a bachelor would not be good for me. So I got married at the age of 49. I do not want to think about what my life would be like without my beautiful wife.

WHY YOU WANT TO KNOW ABOUT ME?

Debbie did not let me get away with anything. Out of all the women I dated, she was the strictest. I could not get away with things the other women ignored.

One day I questioned if she was out with her ex-boyfriend.

Her response was, "Did you see me?"

My response was, "No."

She said, "Do not come to me with foolishness or hearsay."

I never questioned her again.

One day after we returned from a movie, Debbie told me I was not invited upstairs for the evening. I needed clarification. I had never been taught about the complexities of relationships.

She continued, "I decided to become celibate and rededicate my life to Christ."

I said, "Ok," although I did not know what she meant.

I said, "I guess we are celibate."

I called my oldest sister and asked her about celibacy.

I called Debbie the next day and told her I appreciated her honesty, and we remained in touch. I dated different women in the following months, but none of them compared to Debbie.

I heard a voice say, "Go back."

I said, "God. Is she going to take me back?"

God said, "If I tell you to go back, she will take you back."

From that day on, if she said, "Go to church," I would go to church, and sometimes I fell asleep.

I would come in from the casino, shower, and attend church. Every Sunday for a year and a half, I went to Atlantic City after church.

The first time I experienced hearing God's voice, I was in Atlantic City, returning home after losing a lot of money.

I asked God, "Why am I crying so much today?"

God said, "I need you with me now."

He repeated, "I need you to come here with me now." I didn't know what it meant until I got home. I always turn the television to Sports Center. This time when I turned on the television, Prophetess Juanita Bynum preached. I couldn't turn it off. I will never forget that moment. I sat down and listened.

I still get chills now when I think about it.

The prophet finished her sermon, and she said, "I am talking to somebody out there. God is telling you to come in because God has a plan for your life."

I called Debbie's sister Dee Dee up right away. She is a Christian and knows many ministers, televangelists, gospel singers, and prophets. I asked who this lady on tv was. I believed she was talking to me.

Dee Dee said, "That the lady is the prophet."

I said, "God had me listening to a prophet today?"

So Dee Dee explained what a prophet was and what prophesy meant. The message convicted me, and I wanted to change.

I told Debbie, "I do not want to go back to Atlantic City. I decided to give up gambling."

On Sunday, May 14, 2000 (Debbie's birthday and Mother's Day), I proposed to her in the church in front of family members and friends.

She said, "Yes!"

Debbie wanted to be engaged for 1 year, but her mother convinced her we could plan a wedding in 6 months. They wanted 2000 because it was the millennium year.

Debbie's mother said, "You have known each other for 30 years; why wait?" The rest was history and the best decision ever!

WHY YOU WANT TO KNOW ABOUT ME?

During our on-and-off relationship, I maintained a relationship with her mother. I am grateful for her role in my life because she never spoke down to me or judged me.

During the proposal, her pastor said she planted a $25 seed for my salvation. If it were not for her prayers and encouragement to attend church, I would not have had a relationship with God. I do not want to think about where I would be.

Pre-marital counseling ended up being one of the best things for our marriage. The things I learned in counseling prepared me for my wife's cancer diagnosis. When she became sick, I started cleaning, driving, washing dishes, cooking, grocery shopping, and most importantly, caring for my wife.

Before her diagnosis, I believed the only chore men should do was to take out the trash. I had the attitude that I should pay people to do the work I did not want to do.

God is still bringing me a mighty long way. Debbie has been happier for the past few months. Each morning she prays for me. God knew what my life would become.

He allowed me to marry the right woman. I was double blessed by my relationship with God and my marriage to Debbie: the greatest things that ever happened to me.

SHERMAN HARRIS, JR

Saved

*Everyone who calls on the
Name of the Lord will be saved.*
ROMANS 10:13

In 2000, I gave my life to Christ. I became a Christian and abandoned Catholicism. Being raised Catholic, the transition showed me how gracious God was towards me. I believe Jesus Christ died on the cross, was buried, and rose again on the third day for my sins. Despite my limited understanding, I knew God was doing something great in my life.

My decision to become a Christian did not mean that every day would be perfect. It's important to remember that each day is unique and presents its own challenges and opportunities. As a believer, it is important to have faith and trust in Jesus, but it is also important to be prepared for the challenges that may come with that. It is not helpful to frame the challenges as coming from an enemy, as this can lead to a negative and fearful mindset. Instead, focus on the strength and support that can come from your faith. We have to be honest with new believers. What is the problem with telling people that every day will not be perfect? Instead, tell them that each day will be different.

WHY YOU WANT TO KNOW ABOUT ME?

Consider your relationship with God like running track. The runners all come to the line. Everyone stands in their designated lane. If the runner does not move from the starting position, they will not win the race. The same is true for our relationship with God.

Being saved is just the beginning of being a follower of Christ. Now, get ready and prepared for the next step.

The next step is to have a relationship with the right people. You must spend time learning more about the ways of God.

Recently, as I exited the basement, God said, "It is easy to tell the truth, son. It is easy, but you make it difficult! Truth is what sets you free. Whenever you speak the truth and people do not want to listen, you have me, my son!"

In a different conversation with God, I asked Him, "Why are there good people in jail who told the truth?" To this day, I have not received an answer from God; and I have been asking for a while. I know I will receive HIS response, but I am not ready for it. When God knows I am ready, HE will explain everything to me. Perhaps it is what some people must go through in their journey. Like in the Bible, many stories exist about people going through challenges.

For instance, let's look at Jacob's son Joseph. First, he was sold into slavery by his brothers. Then Joseph was falsely accused by his master's wife, which led to his imprisonment. Nevertheless, Joseph maintained his faith and was greatly rewarded. Maybe, this story is relatable for someone who told the truth and was wrongly accused and sent to jail.

I often experienced unhappiness. Money didn't make me happy because I had plenty of it. I constantly sought happiness. I knew something was missing; however, I did not realize what that something was until 2006. I was riding back from Georgia after attending Mega Fest hosted by Bishop T.D. Jakes. During the ride, God revealed the void.

God said, "You are going everywhere to hear preachers, and that is it. You are just going."

God was right. I received many messages but did not have a revelation or understanding. God wanted me to learn to praise and worship Him sincerely.

Everyone must direct their sincere praise to God. The only way to do that is to have a relationship with Him.

Start by asking God, "How do you want me to pray daily?"

Then, "God, how can I praise you today?"

We have been listening to everyone else on how to praise. Being silent before God, listening to music, and reading God's Word are good ways to praise Him. You can praise God any way He wants you to praise Him. Sometimes, God has me sit still and listen instead of being involved in conversations around me.

WHY YOU WANT TO KNOW ABOUT ME?

The Basement

*I had a hunger for God,
And I needed direction.*
SHERMAN HARRIS, JR.

From 2000 - 2004, my routine, once Debbie left for work, was to enter the basement to pray and worship. Once Debbie came home from work, I immediately came upstairs for dinner, and we discussed her day. After dinner, I returned to the basement to pray and read the Bible. My hunger for God was strong, and I believe He knew it!

Debbie understood God was working on me when I spent time in the basement. I was so constant that I had to relearn how to spend time with my wife. Debbie has been gracious in putting up with me and my new behaviors. We spent most of our time together on weekends.

During this period, I desperately sought God's guidance and direction, I did not want to continue to have financial ties to my past, so I refused to accept payments from the club.

My hunger for God was so strong that I wanted to stay in His presence. I listened to all types of gospel music and watched different televangelists daily. I never got tired of learning more about God and His ways. I cried during this period, and I never knew why.

We need to know when God speaks to us versus the flesh or the world. I would use this analogy. God will speak to you in your language. I know when I hear His voice, it is always the same. Some people receive messages through music, dreams, nature, people, etc. I learned to hear the voice of God during my prayer, praise, and worship in the basement.

WHY YOU WANT TO KNOW ABOUT ME?

Humbled

Humble yourselves before the Lord,
And He will lift you up.
JAMES 4:10

In 2004, God led me to work at Target. I was humbled. On the first day, I went for an interview with the managers' Pam and Margaret; as the interview continued, I said, "Ma'am, I do not want to scare you, but God told me I already have the job."

Once we completed the paperwork, I signed it. The manager informed me she had to get the main hiring manager. I informed her that she could but that I would be at work on Monday. She laughed and said, we are hiring eleven people. She went and got the hiring manager in; she said, "you told Pam you already have the job?"

I said, "Yes, ma'am. You will call to tell me that I must come in on Monday."

She said, "How did you know?"

I said, "I don't know, but God knows."

She said, "I do not believe in God. I am an atheist."

I said, "Before I leave this job, you will know God. That is why God sent me here. I have the job. Y'all take care."

I walked out of the door.

They called on Friday evening at 5 o'clock and told me to come on Monday at 9.

I came in Monday morning, and my career began at Target. When I entered, Pam started laughing when she saw me. She said, "We want to start you off at the highest hourly rate."

I said, "No, that's wrong too."

She replied, "What is it now?"

I asked, "What is your lowest rate?

She said, "It is $8.40."

I pleaded, "That is it. I must start up $8.40."

She said, "I have never heard anyone say they want to be paid less."

I said, "Well, ma'am, I don't want less, but God told me to do that. I must come in to humble myself. Then, after 2 months, you can give me the increase."

She said, "Are you sure?"

I said, "I am positive."

I was paid $8.40 per hour for 2 months. I came home and cried to Debbie because my pay for 2 weeks was only $488.

I never cashed the checks; I automatically gave them to Debbie to deposit in the bank. I kept $88 and gave $100 to the church every Sunday. When I started making $1200 every 2 weeks, I gave $150 for my tithes. I realized I could never pay too much for what God did for me. I became addicted to giving.

I resigned from Target in 2006, just shy of my 2nd anniversary. One Sunday, I asked Debbie to give me $100 for my tithes. I never stopped giving despite my lack of income. Debbie informed me that she did not have $100 at the time and gave me $50. I did not speak to her all the way home. God beat me up about my response to my wife. I apologized for my behavior.

WHY YOU WANT TO KNOW ABOUT ME?

God said, "Why would you get upset with her because you are not working? I know you are humble, and I know your heart."

SHERMAN HARRIS, JR

Prayer Still Works

*I asked God to take the thoughts
away before I got married.*
SHERMAN HARRIS, JR.

Before I married Debbie, I asked God to help me honor my marriage vows. My parents were a great example of marriage. Nothing but death separated them.

I asked God to give me a woman that loved me as much as I loved her. Next, I desired help to stay committed and honor my vows. My second prayer was to take the desire to gamble away. I recognized my marriage would not work if I was out gambling. If He could not help me overcome my desire for women and to gamble, I did not want to get married.

Before I got married, I still thought about some of the other girls sometimes. I asked God to take the thoughts away before I married because I did not want to hold on to the past. The day I returned from vacation; I was tempted by a phone call I received from a young lady.

I said, "Where are you?" She told me where she was. I got in the car and headed in the direction of the location.

WHY YOU WANT TO KNOW ABOUT ME?

I could not find the street. I turned back around. When I turned back around, the vehicle was facing toward the direction of my house. She called me again on the phone. I told her.

"I can't make it. This relationship is over."

The voice of God told me as clear as day, "I told you I am going to protect you."

From that day on, my desire for other women was gone. It was like God erased that desire from me. I was a new person —no desire for any woman other than my wife.

I was tested again when my wife was diagnosed with cancer. I can honestly say that I had no desire when she was sick while undergoing chemotherapy. I wanted to ensure she received everything she needed. I learned to enjoy cuddling and caring for her every need. I went 9 months and had no desire for another woman—no pornographic movies or magazines.

Our relationship grew closer.

I see women daily, but it does not mean anything to me. I recall a time I went to Las Vegas with Big Mike. My wife and I still laugh about this story to this day. I started watching Big Mike play when I stopped gambling.

Two females were playing as well. I was holding $10,000 of his winnings, and he won another $5000, bringing his winnings to $15,000. I asked him if he wanted me to cash it in, and he said, "yes." When I returned, one of the ladies asked Mike, "Who is your friend?"

He said, "He's happily married and is not interested."

She said, "Well, will he talk?"

He said, "Yeah, go ahead and try."

When I returned to the table, she asked, "Is there any way I can come to your room?"

I asked her, "Are you a call girl? Because if you are a call girl, that will not work. I'll tell you what you can do. Can you read scriptures?"

She said, "I just like to give massages."

She continued, "I just like listening to him talk."

I responded, "Well, yeah, it's a good conversation about those scriptures. That is all it is going to be. If you can read scriptures, then you can come upstairs."

I gave her the room number and told her to come up when she was ready to read the scriptures, but she never showed up.

Mike asked me what would happen if she came up to read the scriptures. She would have to leave after she read the scriptures. Mike used to tell me how blessed I am to find someone like Debbie, and I wish I could be as strong as you

As men, I feel sometimes we allow pretty women to tempt us. Do not allow temptation and beauty to take you away from your relationship. If you have a 100% relationship built on love, why would you sacrifice the 100% for 20% one-night fling? The 20% may represent the areas of weakness or deficit in your relationship. We all have them. No one is perfect. Regardless, it is not worth losing 80% for 20%.

Mike has a nightclub in Atlanta. One day I was sitting beside the stage, praying for the people there. A young lady approached me and said, "Sir, are you praying?"

I said, "What makes you think I am praying?"

She said, "That look on your face. I thank you for praying for me. I mean it."

That is when God allowed me to pray and give her prophetic word.

She walked over and asked Big Mike, "Did you tell him I was interested in the medical field?" Big Mike confirmed he did not have an opportunity to discuss her. However, she was astonished because God revealed that she was studying and wanted to be a nurse.

I said, "You have been distracted. That is why you have not been studying."

The girl looked at me and started to cry. She asked if she could hug me, and I said yes. As she hugged me, she informed Big Mike she was going home. A few months later, he heard from her; she had completed her degree in nursing.

I am a living witness to the power of prayer.

Part Three:

The Turnaround

WHY YOU WANT TO KNOW ABOUT ME?

Passion for Fashion

*I loved fashion, and I wanted
to do something different
than what was shown during that time.*
SHERMAN HARRIS, JR.

My passion for fashion was influenced by the older gentlemen in my neighborhood during high school. I was never into fads or trends and never liked wearing designer clothes; I preferred my style. I always wore white in the summertime; my favorite summer outfit was a white warm-up suit. One of my buddies and I started wearing silk shirts, dress slacks (no jeans), and nice quality shoes. This trend continued throughout my adult life. In the winter, you could find me dressed to the nines with a brimmed hat and a leather coat.

My passion for fashion would re-emerge later in life when I created Javiere Modeling in 1998 with 16 young ladies. A hip-hop mogul and his bride were the coveted duos of the latest fashion brands, and I had the best models to represent their brands on the runway when they came to the DMV. I decided early the models would avoid wearing lingerie or swimwear in our fashion shows. Some of the young ladies had previous modeling experience, and coaching was provided for those that needed additional support. Over time 42 diverse models graced the runways. One of the models was chosen for a national beverage campaign. She shot the commercial and was preparing for a twelve-state press tour when she found out she was pregnant.

I had a great relationship with one of the leading urban fashion designers for seven years. I wanted to instill in the young ladies my principles that you can still have style and grace and look good without wearing swimwear and lingerie. I wanted to show the young ladies they could model the latest fashions and be classy without exposing their bodies. My goal was to ensure the parents felt comfortable with the selection of clothing being modeled.

Some years later, several fathers approached and thanked me for the encouragement and prayers for their daughters. One young lady admitted she could have avoided some situations in her life, if she had listened to my advice. I encouraged her to view her situation as a learning experience.

The coach and mentor in me continues to encourage young ladies as they go through their journey in life. They are amazed by the information I shared with them from God. Some listened, some did not, and were humble enough to admit it later.

The biggest blessings from my modeling agency were meeting two parents: Mrs. Kershaw and Mrs. Walton. They helped me in my business and introduced me to their pastor and church family in 2003. Both ladies invited me at different points, but Mrs. Kershaw insisted I visit because she wanted me to meet her Pastor, Leonard Lacey. After we visited the first time, Debbie and I knew we had found our church home. The Sunday, they opened in the new building in Stafford, Virginia; Debbie and I were the first members to join United Faith Christian Ministry.

WHY YOU WANT TO KNOW ABOUT ME?

In 2001, Chris and I rented a building on 8th Street in Washington, DC, and opened a clothing store called *Just Phashun*. We enjoyed traveling to New York to purchase the latest trendy garments. We arrived from New York on Thursday and restocked the store just in time for the weekend shoppers. Unfortunately, we opened the store Friday morning and discovered the merchandise was gone. The business was thriving, but the store was broken into every other month. With such frequent thefts, the business suffered due to the consistent loss of revenue and my soft heart.

I had an ice cream truck for a few years. I tried to drive the truck for a few months but was unsuccessful because I gave away more ice cream than I sold. In addition, I felt bad if the kids did not have money. That business quickly dissolved, but these setbacks did not stop me from pursuing other entrepreneurial endeavors. Sometimes in life, we make bad choices; however, God still loves and forgives us. Have you read about all the mistakes I made?

SHERMAN HARRIS, JR

Javiere

*The name Javiere
spoke peace and love to me.*
SHERMAN HARRIS, JR.

Javiere was a name that instantly spoke peace and love to me. The name was used across multiple businesses, including a modeling agency and, eventually, a home renovation business. My next business endeavor was brought to my attention by a friend of mine, Nathan, who was a real estate investor. I received a call from Nathan asking if I would like to oversee his business while he was out of town. When he returned, he asked me how the guys completed their duties. I reported that some of the guys worked hard up until lunchtime, and after a liquid lunch, it was all downhill.

After Nathan asked me to oversee his operations on numerous occasions, he recommended I go to Home Depot and start hiring my crew. Nathan said, "I have 350 houses, and I will keep you busy."

I took him up on his suggestion and recruited a few guys for my crew. I suffered a few setbacks; however, it was a learning experience and the best thing to happen as I started a business, Javiere Home Solutions. The Holy Spirit spoke to me about obtaining my Class C license. I was thrilled to have the authority to legally provide contractual services for less than $10,000 each and no more than $150,000 annually. Javiere Home Solutions was formed in 2009.

My brother Lenny introduced me to a property management company that hired us for small jobs. After developing a relationship with the property manager, I obtained more work which, in turn, resulted in me obtaining my Class A license. This license enabled me to accept larger contracts with the company. Once I got my Class A in 2010, I never looked back. What started early as a setback was God preparing the way for me.

It reminds me of Genesis 50:20 (NIV):
> *"You intended to harm me, but God intended it for good to accomplish what is now being done, the saving of many lives."*

If I had kept working for Nathan, I would have never pursued my license and obtained my own business because he kept me busy. The first thing the property management company asked me was if I was insured. I realized, at that time, that I was playing a different ball game. I got licensed and bonded. It was a good thing. Look at God!

I currently have 14 employees. I have learned to shift employees to handle the work requirements based on the workload. I consider it a blessing to be able to do the work that I do with my team.

SHERMAN HARRIS, JR

Oh, Brother

"There's no other love like the love for a brother.
There's no other love like the love from a brother."
Astrid Alauda

Lenny was a father, husband, and activist, but to me, he was my brother. We did everything together, from coaching teams to our entrepreneurial endeavors. Lenny was strong in his beliefs. He did not allow anyone to speak to him in a condescending manner or insult his intelligence. Lenny did not play. He did not take any mess from anyone.

My brother and I vacationed and traveled to the Men's Apparel Guild in California (MAGIC) Fashion Trade Show Las Vegas, the largest apparel showcase from around the world. We shared the excitement of shopping for items for our clothing stores. Lenny and I traveled to various trade shows, attended seminars, and purchased the latest items for our retail store. We enjoyed spending time together.

Lenny established his own extermination business and worked diligently to carefully formulate the right chemical combination to rid the apartment complex tenants of bed bugs. Once, a client asked him for his formula.

WHY YOU WANT TO KNOW ABOUT ME?

The client asked him what he used to treat bedbugs.

His reply was, "why would I tell you that? If I tell you what I used, you will not need me. I think that is disrespectful. So, I would appreciate it if you would not ask me that again."

He introduced me to a property management company I still work with to this day.

When I think about it, Lenny was our father's favorite. After high school, my father co-signed for me to get a truck, and I made the payments. There came a point when I wanted to get rid of the truck.

Dad insisted I give the truck to Lenny.

I thought, "Yeah, Lenny is his favorite."

He always told me to take care of my brother Lenny. My father left me with these words:

> "You are going to be okay. But I need you to take care of your siblings. I know you will not like it sometimes, but I need you to look after them."

The words of my father continue to echo in my life today.

As close as we were, I did not know Lenny was an activist. I thought he was just attending support group meetings. I had no idea he was advocating for others. My brother was always busy helping people.

I learned much more about my brother after he was listed as missing. With each passing day, we learned more about him. All the local news outlets were present at my brother's funeral and every night during the trial of his killers. I just stopped commenting.

I had to say, "No, I'm not doing it anymore."

It was just too difficult to process his senseless murder. It was also strange to see the reaction of well-intended people, especially church people.

I know we do not like it when tragedy strikes. If we live long enough, no one is exempt from grief. But we must believe in God, even in bad times. Know that nothing catches God by surprise. When my brother was robbed and killed, it was a devastating loss.

Just like with my family, it was hard to grasp based on the circumstances surrounding this situation. We think about the horrific tragedy, but the reality is we all are going to die. So, if my brother died in his sleep or passed away in a car accident, he is still gone. I am not trying to be cruel, but death is one appointment we all will face. We do not know the day or the time, but we know where we are going.

Aside from losing my parents, the loss of my brother is one of my greatest losses. It is not the fact that he died. It was the senseless act that led to his death. My love for my brother will never die. A prophet called to offer condolences and told me Lenny would be found within five days, near water. Approximately five days later, we received a phone call that Lenny's body was found. The prophet was right, as he was many other times before.

WHY YOU WANT TO KNOW ABOUT ME?

The Prophet

*"Before I formed you in the womb I knew you,
before you were born, I set you apart.
I appointed you as prophet to the nations".*
JEREMIAH 1:5 (NIV)

Years ago, a lady gave me a prophetic word. She said, "You have a gift many people will not understand. God will allow you to see and hear many things in the past, present, and future, and God will also give you an understanding and bless you with a gift of prophecy. You are a seer and a prophet."

I asked Debbie what that meant, and we consulted her sister Dee Dee, who explained in detail. Looking back, everything prophesied to me in 2001 has come to pass.

In 2006, I visited a church in North Carolina, and the pastor prophesied over six people. Then he informed the congregation there was one more he had to reach. There were 300 - 400 people in the congregation, and the prophet came in my direction (God revealed he was coming to me).

Sure enough, the pastor came straight to me. God instructed me to listen to the message. To date, I remember this message verbatim:

"You are worried because you are not a great reader or speller. God will use you how He sees fit. Just be obedient and watch what God does. You are going to do something that will shock the world. Just be patient!"

I hung on to God's every word and prayed for clarity.

God gave the title of this book: *"Why you want to know about me?"*

I asked God, "What do you mean?"

He told me, "I will give you the words to say."

I want to do what He says, as He instructed me. I do not want to hide any of my life's details, including gambling, hustling, and women. But there's also growth.

I do not pray and study as much as I did in the past, but God still empowers me with this gift. Rev. Samuels, our Assistant Pastor, told me that the time spent in the basement was a time of preparation. God knew the business would get inundated with jobs at times. God still blesses me, despite the lack of prayer and study. I feel I'm cheating God because I do not give Him enough quality time. He unfailingly shows up for me, and God is always on time!

Sometimes after my speaking engagements, over a dozen people want to speak with me. For example, identical twins were in attendance, and God gave me a word of prophecy for one and a prayer for the other. The one that received prayer was upset because her sister received a word of prophecy, and she did not.

I told her, "God told me to pray for you. Don't you know how powerful that is? Think about it, sweetheart. God allowed me to pray for you. But, if you listened to the prayer, He also prophesied to you."

WHY YOU WANT TO KNOW ABOUT ME?

As I left, a lady came running outside of church and asked, "Prophet, can you tell me how my job is going this week?"

I said, "Ma'am, I'm not in the business of fortune telling. I can only say what He tells me. Right now, God has not given me anything to say, but I can pray for you. Would you like for me to pray for you?"

She responded, "No. I just wanted to see if you knew because you prophesied to everyone else."

I interrupted her, "God did not instruct me to prophesy to everyone."

Debbie thought my tone was a little rough on the lady.

I realized that not everyone is ready to receive one. Attendance increases significantly when a prophet is announced or promoted at a church. People will come out in droves to get a prophecy, but they will not spend time with God to get a revelation.

Often people advise me, days or months later, that the prophecy I spoke over them came to pass. I did my job as a man of God. As God's messenger, I delivered the mail.

It is okay if someone informs me the prophecy is fulfilled, but I do not want people to feel obligated to tell me when God does what He does. I know it will be fulfilled. God will deliver as He promised. Therefore, I follow God's guidance to do nothing more, nothing less.

Recently, I visited a church where a prophet prophesied to three people and went to a fourth person. God revealed to me that the prophet guessed the fourth person. You should only speak what God gives you. When God speaks, He is clear.

While traveling, I experienced a prophet guessing at delivering a prophecy on me. I left my wedding ring in the hotel room. The prophet informed me my marriage would be restored; however, it was already intact.

Take horoscopes as an example. Some Christians read and believe in them. I have read horoscopes before, and the messages never apply to me. Gypsies may have some great gifts, but they use their gifts to earn a living.

At first, I did not always believe in the gift of prophecy. Debbie and I arrived at church one Sunday and were immediately called into the pastor's office. The pastor relayed the conversation we had while driving to church. Previously I thought Debbie and my sister-in-law were telling our business. At that time, I was still gambling, and the prophet knew all the details of my business. He was and is a powerful man of God with a true gift of prophecy. Gifts are without repentance. Try the Spirit by the Spirit and determine what is of God and what is of man.

Recently, I visited another church, and they asked all the prophets to stand.

I said to Debbie, "Look at this."

I stood up fast! After the service, people approached me and began to ask questions. Three ladies came to me, and the Spirit led me to tell them to give their phone numbers to my wife. Debbie informed them I would give them a call when God leads me. I was thrilled to see my wife operating in her gift of encouragement and support for me. Debbie asked if I followed up with the ladies; I told her I would only speak to a female with her or another female in the ministry being present.

WHY YOU WANT TO KNOW ABOUT ME?

Pop Up Prayer

You cannot go big,
without growing small!
SHERMAN HARRIS, JR.

God has instructed me to pop up and pray at different places. So, I call it "Pop Up Prayer!" I was asked if I would promote Pop Up Prayer, and I told them I would wait until God instructs me.

Recently, God led me to pray for Chick-fil-A locations, their owners, managers, and team members. Now God has revealed; now it is time for churches. I received a request from a bishop friend to launch at his church, but God did not instruct me on when or where to begin. If I do not proceed as God wants, it will not work.

I feel God is leading me toward smaller congregations first, but I do not know where He is leading me. You cannot go big without growing small! He said, the first shall be last, and the last shall be first.

Someone told me, "You are getting ready to get large, and how will you handle it?

I replied, "I do not know, but I will tell you; I will always do what God leads me."

SHERMAN HARRIS, JR

I depend on God; He keeps me humble. I know that I know that I know, it is not me! It is the God in me. I will continue to pop up and pray as God leads me. It may be at a restaurant or at a church, but regardless of the location, I will be ready.

WHY YOU WANT TO KNOW ABOUT ME?

The Favor of God

*The fear of the Lord is the beginning of wisdom,
and knowledge of the Holy One is understanding.*
Proverbs 9:10 (NIV)

God has been so good to me. When I look back on my past to where He has brought me, from the streets and having a successful business, it brings tears to my eyes. I believe the statement, "favor ain't fair."

I recognize the favor of God in my life. God is so good. My priorities are to ensure my wife, household, and extended family has what they need.

Debbie is the big reason I established a relationship with God. For years, Debbie planted a $25 seed for my salvation. I was double blessed by coming into a relationship with Debbie. She planted the seed, and God allowed me to marry her. We have been married for over 22 years in a successful marriage, and we only had one argument about my tone in front of others. She extended me grace, and we did not go to bed angry. We should understand that communication is key to every relationship (marriage, friendship, business, etc.). We should always sit down and talk about issues; if not, the slightest little disagreement can become a major argument.

Only God can sustain our marriage. I know there are things about me she does not like and vice versa.

For instance, one day, I raised my voice at Debbie, and other people were nearby. She gave me a look, and I asked her what was wrong. She said we would discuss it later and to lower my voice.

The way she said it, I knew I had to get it together. I toned it down. Once we got in the car, we talked about what had happened.

I have learned that you can argue every day if you choose to. So Debbie and I choose not to. It is that simple. I can't explain it, but God has been so good to us.

God covered me for eight years while I was gambling, hustling, and managing exotic dancers, which made me a lot of money. During that time, I did not experience problems with the police, robberies, or physical harm. I am forever grateful for His protection, and every day I will give Him honor by being obedient.

To show you how God worked, in the past, I prayed with the guys every morning. One morning, I gave a word of prophecy to someone that they would have problems with their boss. I encouraged him to do the following when speaking with the boss:

1. Don't get offended.
2. Listen to your boss and be prepared; they may say something you may not like, but remember, God is testing you to see how strong you are to handle the situation.
3. After you pass the test, you will get a raise in 2 -3 months.

They called me a couple of weeks later, screaming, "Sherman, not that I did not believe you, but I got a raise today."

WHY YOU WANT TO KNOW ABOUT ME?

They said, "Thanks for your encouragement and instruction because I may not have responded appropriately."

I said, "God led you to make the right decision. God sent me as a messenger to warn you, and you listened. As a result, you were rewarded, which is important."

Sometimes you may not like the message, but listening is necessary!

SHERMAN HARRIS, JR

God Is Always Right

*God never makes a mistake,
and He will not wait to get to me
or you to start.*
SHERMAN HARRIS

One morning while visiting a Chick-fil-A, I noticed extremely long lines. I informed the young lady at the window of the revelation I received while waiting. "There is a staff shortage because management is not doing their job."

One manager was doing the work of four people. She was stressed out and in tears. I got out of the car and walked in to speak with her. She shared her health concerns and staffing issues. I encouraged her to share her observations with management, prophesying they would be efficiently staffed within five days.

Shortly after, I returned to this location, and service times were improved. When I pulled to the drive-thru, the young lady said, "That's him! He's out there. Thank you for what you did for this Chick-fil-A. What you told us, we told our boss, and he wants to see you."

I told her, "God said it. God is always right."

On another occasion, I went through the drive-thru, and the team offered me a free grilled chicken and egg-white sandwich. I told

WHY YOU WANT TO KNOW ABOUT ME?

them I wanted to pay for my meal. I do not want anyone to think I am using God's gift for personal benefit.

Once I speak God's Word, my job is done. God never makes a mistake, and He will not wait for me or you to start. God is always right. Even when I pondered why God gave me the title, *Why You Want to Know About Me*? I thought, is it about me, God, or my transition with God?

I know He wants me to share where He brought me from to the present. Even though I am not always right, God is always right.

SHERMAN HARRIS, JR

The Gifts Are Without Repentance

*For the gifts and calling
of God are without repentance.*
ROMANS 11:29 (NIV)

I subcontracted someone to do a large project. Unfortunately, he received half of the monies, then abandoned the job. He did not fulfill his obligation, yet I was responsible for completing the job to fulfill my contractual obligations. The company told me they could find someone else to finish the job, but I would no longer be allowed to work with them as a contractor. Please be mindful that most of my business is with this company. It was a no-brainer for me. I had to fulfill my contractual obligation for the project.

Immediately after, I went to the casino in West Virginia. I thought I could win it back because I used to win big when I played. After 19 years, I started gambling again, trying to recoup the money I lost from the contract.

So, I began to sneak away from the house. I felt uncomfortable being dishonest with Debbie, but she knew something was wrong because whenever she asked me where I was, I changed the subject. I did not lie, but I did not answer the question. Debbie is so smart; I cannot get anything over on her.

WHY YOU WANT TO KNOW ABOUT ME?

She asked me when I got home, "I noticed you did not want to tell me where you were. Are you okay?"

I did not want to start lying to my wife. We have a beautiful marriage, and I did not want to do anything to jeopardize our relationship. So, I told her I was in West Virginia gambling.

She said, "Please be careful, honey."

Debbie has been with me 100%, even when I lost a lot of money in various situations. She pointed out that I never get angry or speak about my losses, but she pays attention when I get quiet.

She said, "I just thank God because most men would have a different response if someone took that much money from them."

Her response blew my mind. I eventually realized gambling would not help me get the money back. Only God could restore what was lost. I went to God and cried out for help. On my birthday, September 30, 2019, I told God I wanted this to be my last day gambling.

Please do not think I am justifying my actions. While gambling is legal, too much of anything is not good. What makes gambling wrong is when you take the money set aside to pay your mortgage and utilities to spend it gambling. Anything not done in moderation is unwise. The key is to have self-control which means sticking to a budget. On the flip side, there are busloads of church people going to Atlantic City daily while preachers tell us we're going to hell if we go to the casino and play the lottery. That is terrible advice.

In 2020, stay-at-home orders were issued worldwide due to COVID. Everything was on lockdown. God shut the entire world down. I think God intervened to ensure I did not go back to gambling. God loves me so much; He assured me I would never return.

SHERMAN HARRIS, JR

Why would God continue to bless me while gambling? My vision and anointing became stronger during this time. That is backward. I guess it's why God is God. I was in a casino, and God continued to give me wisdom and His knowledge. He allowed me to see things and share Him with others. Gifts are without repentance. I am still a work in progress, but I thank God for being patient with me.

WHY YOU WANT TO KNOW ABOUT ME?

Iron Sharpens Iron

As iron sharpens iron,
so one person sharpens another.
PROVERBS 27:17 (NIV)

God has given me a ministry for men to come together each Monday at 6 a.m., a power-packed hour or so forum via conference call. We have guys participating from New York to South Carolina. As a reminder to anyone who joins, it is not a church-like atmosphere. The individuals selected are chosen by God, through me, to share the weekly discussion.

The men have shared how they have been blessed by the nuggets shared during our time together. Since the beginning, I have seen much growth from the men. Our sessions provide insight into life. There are no topics off-limits. We are about improving ourselves. During these sessions, God gives wisdom and instruction. Participation is not mandatory, but it is recommended that we listen to those who do not feel comfortable sharing about themselves.

I want people around me that are sharper than me. Iron sharpens iron is not just for the men I serve but also for me. For example, several years ago, I arrived at the home of Mr. Oweis, a seasoned senior in Chantilly, Virginia, to estimate a home renovation. Upon meeting Mr. Oweis, I received a phone call and briefly spoke to the caller. Then, I introduced myself and provided the requested estimate.

Mr. Oweis stated, "The check is blank; whatever you put on there is okay with me. I overheard your call when you said, '*it is easier, to tell the truth.*' When I overheard your statement, you immediately gained my trust."

I completed the work on his basement, and he never questioned the price. Mr. Oweis showed me how I saved him a lot of money from previous quotes from other companies. God connected us because I had no idea, we would become friends. We meet every Tuesday morning for breakfast and have done so for the past six years. He is a man of great insight and wisdom. He is a walking archive of local history. I enjoy listening to all the information he shares. He is a retired professor with over 42 years of classroom service.

When Mr. Oweis and I first met, he teared up during our talks and when we departed. Our conversations are very special as I have gained a lot of wisdom and knowledge in our time together.

Just because I am a prophet does not mean I cannot learn something, as this relationship with Mr. Oweis provides an example.

I love to see spiritual growth in others. I love to watch others grow in God. If you do not go through something, you cannot get there. You got there because of what you go through. When teaching or preaching takes place, the vessel should have already been ministered to deliver the Word; when you go through it, the Word comes alive. You cannot teach anything you have not gone through. But once you go through you can teach it well.

WHY YOU WANT TO KNOW ABOUT ME?

The opposite of iron sharpens iron would be repeating what is heard and never experiencing what they are sharing.

Everyone is doing what they see other people doing. Talking about what God said to them, and none of it was working. God is always right. You will know the truth, and the truth will set you free.

God gave me my prophetic gift to encourage, correct, and bless. Are you willing to be corrected? That is only a question you can answer. I am not going to say something to make you feel good because I do not want to receive punishment from God. As I stated previously, I will only say what God says. *Iron Sharpens Iron* is an open forum for men to share their stories to help each other navigate life.

SHERMAN HARRIS, JR

Bring Jesus Back

*I don't know when God
will turn things around,
but I know that He will.*
SHERMAN HARRIS, JR.

I would like to have the opportunity to speak with some of the leading television evangelists, such as T.D. Jakes, Charles Stanley, Joseph Prince, and Joel Osteen, just to name a few. I want to talk to them because I have a fresh Rhema from God for each of them. So the first question I want to ask them is, "When are we going to start using the name Jesus on television?"

The Bible says we can't get to the Father without going through Jesus.

John 14:6 (NIV):

> "Jesus answered, I am the way and the truth, and the life. No one can come to the Father except through me."

It is time to bring back the name of Jesus to the forefront. The name *god* can be used for any idol. God has brought this to my attention, and I want to do what He has asked me to do.

WHY YOU WANT TO KNOW ABOUT ME?

I Am Not Jesus, But You Can Thank Jesus

The Father and I are one.

JOHN 10:30 (NIV)

Some years ago, I spoke at a Latino church in Annandale, Virginia. Over time the attendance grew from 40 in attendance to over 200. Then, I stopped visiting because I felt they began to worship me. They acted as if Jesus came down through me.

The little girl said to me, "you are Jesus. You saved my family. My mother and my father are not the same anymore. Thank you, Jesus."

I told her, "I am not Jesus, but you can thank Jesus. My sister is 12 years old and has men in the room. You knew that. How did you know that?

I told the parents and the sister to come to the front. I told her, "There will never be another man in your room again in the mighty name of Jesus."

The little girl said, "I know he's right. I have seen them in the room. How did he know? He's Jesus. He's Jesus."

At another service, the little girl ran to me and hugged me as soon as I came in. The little girl said, "I'm so glad God showed up."

I said, "what did you say, sweetheart?"

She said, "God sent you here. You are God for us. You saved my mother. You have changed my mother and my father. You told my father that he would never raise his hand at my mother again in the mighty name of Jesus."

The little girl continued to share that her father raised his hand to strike her mother, and his hand became locked, and he could not lower his hand. When the ambulance assisted him, a church member asked if I could "take it off him."

The mother explained that when he reached back to strike, he could not hit her. I informed her that I could not do anything. Only God can handle the situation. I just told the father to stop hitting you. I was informed that it took three days for his hand to come down. I said the Father, the Son, and the Holy Spirit were at work in his life. The father gave his life to Christ and is now a preacher.

WHY YOU WANT TO KNOW ABOUT ME?

Growth

Growth happens; expect it to occur.

Sherman Harris, Jr.

When I started operating in my prophetic gift. I was excited to share what God revealed to me. However, there were times when people did not receive the message, and I learned to wait for God to allow me the opportunity to impart His message. I now have enough wisdom to know the appropriate time to release the message.

God taught me how to listen to His voice, and when the time was right, He allowed me to deliver a prophetic message in the right tone and context. When I follow God's flow, I can speak the way He wants me to.

Admittedly, I get excited and rush the message by talking fast, especially when I share good news. However, I am still growing in my gift. Growth happens; expect it to occur. God has shown me some things in the past few months that have given me a different outlook on each day.

Debbie recently reminded me that I ministered on this topic, *"Your Days Can Be Greater."*

I said, "Yeah, God gave it to me, but I did not apply it to my life."

I believe whatever message God gives is for me before I share it with anyone else. The same is true for you. If God gives you a message to impart, it is for you first. If preachers learn to accept what God reveals, the preached word will come with great clarity, and God will be pleased.

One of my favorite passages is Psalm 119:8-16 (NIV)

> "I will obey your decrees; do not utterly forsake me. How can a young person stay on the path of purity? By living according to your word. I seek you with all my heart; do not let me stray from your commands. I have hidden your word so that I might not sin against you. Praise be to you, LORD; teach me your decrees. With my lips I recount all the laws that come from your mouth. I rejoice in following your statutes as one rejoices in great riches. I meditate on your precepts and consider your ways. I delight in your decrees; I will not neglect your word."

I read these scriptures when I need to hear from God. I encourage you to read and listen to these scriptures. What is your favorite scripture? We all need a daily Word from God. Most people think they need prayer. Prayer is important, but God's word carries us through difficult times. What difficult situation are you facing? What areas are you seeking an understanding? What are you trying to obtain? The answers to your questions are found in the Bible. After you read and receive God's Word, you can pray without ceasing. My spiritual growth occurred when I learned to read and apply the scriptures to my life.

WHY YOU WANT TO KNOW ABOUT ME?

Psalm 51:4 (NIV) was a game-changer for me,

> *"Against you, you only have I sinned and done what is evil in your sight."*

God showed me that when I sin, it is not against others; I sin against Him. Now I understand the magnitude of sin; it changed everything. When you fully understand this, you will not stay the same. That does not mean you will not have any issues and struggles, but you will begin to see things differently.

Things that once frustrated me no longer phase me. I tell myself, "God is not messed up about this mess."

God is so graceful, merciful, and forgiving towards us. Unfortunately, we do not always know how to forgive. A sign of unforgiveness is when hearing a particular name brings about a negative emotion. Let it go! Someone once said forgiveness is not for the other person but for you. Letting go is a sign of growth. Continue to read and study for continued growth in God.

SHERMAN HARRIS, JR

Pay Attention

*Do not be so busy looking
at what God is doing for others.
Pay attention to what
He is doing in your life.*
SHERMAN HARRIS, JR.

Months before the pandemic outbreak, God allowed me to pray for the church. I prayed for four consecutive Sundays after everyone left the church. As a seer and prophet, God shows me things months in advance. Seeing things about people I know and care about is difficult, but I enjoy blessing the people of God. I have learned to be obedient and to do as God instructs me.

Do not be so busy looking at what God is doing for others and pay attention to what He is doing in your life. There is nothing wrong with getting ideas from others, but take the time and give your ideas to God. What works for some may not work for others. Stop worrying about what others are doing and wait for God to show you what to do. This applies to leadership as well. Communication and teamwork are important. There are great blessings if you listen to what God is saying.

WHY YOU WANT TO KNOW ABOUT ME?

"Whoever has ears, let them hear." Matthew 11:15 NIV

God will use whomever He wants to get the Word out.

I attended a funeral, and the pastor asked all pastors, prophets, and apostles to please stand. I was sitting there, almost like someone had lifted my jacket. My body felt lifted, and I stood up. After church, a few people came to me.

One elderly lady said to me, "You are the prophet."

I smiled.

She asked, "Why are you smiling?"

I said, "It is the joy of God. I love how God allows you and me to see things. No one told you who I was; I just stood up."

I continued, "You didn't know anything about me."

She said, "May God continue to keep you and use you, son."

I hugged her and said, "May God continue to give you more days."

She said, "Thank you," and walked away. It was refreshing to receive encouragement from a stranger. God is always speaking; we must pay attention.

One day my wife and I were at the grocery store, and a lady approached me and said, "I know God gave you a word for me today."

As I prayed, she broke into tears.

After the prayer, she asked Debbie, "Is it hard for you to have a husband like that? I ask because so many people will be calling your husband. God is preparing to take him higher. Are you going to be able to handle it?"

Debbie said, "I am glad he is paying attention to what God is telling him to do."

SHERMAN HARRIS, JR

God Did It

God does everything for me.

SHERMAN HARRIS, JR.

A powerful woman of God is doing great work for the Kingdom. She is operating in her gift and receiving many accolades and abundant blessings. I pray she does not get caught up in her flesh. She has allowed the praises of men to affect her, making the ministry about her. I participate in a prayer call with her three days a week. I have heard her say things that are not right, so I asked God, "What do you want me to do? What would you have me say to her?"

Recently during a prayer call, she commented on everything she was doing for others. Then, she caught herself and said, "I know the prophet is on the phone, and he always says, '*God said, or God did,*' so let me correct myself. God did it."

I added, "Make no mistake, God does everything for me. I'm not ashamed to say it is Him."

I acknowledge that God is the giver of every good and perfect gift. I do not want anyone to think I am the one speaking when I am

WHY YOU WANT TO KNOW ABOUT ME?

following His guidance. For example, during a call with a friend, I shared scripture with her about her specific situation.

She said, "Didn't you say you were driving? So how did you know this scripture applied to our conversation?"

I said, "Because God gave it to me to give to you."

Another example is when I attended a funeral, a set of identical twins approached me. One of them asked, "Do you remember five years ago you prophesied to me?"

I responded, "no, ma'am."

To jog my memory, one of them said, "They always call me the good twin and call her the bad twin, and you told us to stop calling her bad. Since that day, people have no longer called us good or bad."

She continued, "I was jealous because you whispered and told my sister something. So, she told me what you said."

I admitted I often whisper God's message to the person because He does not allow me to embarrass anyone.

She said, "You nailed it right on the button."

I corrected her, "I didn't know, but God knew."

They testified how God opened doors for them to own an antique shop and went on and on about how God blessed them after they received the prophetic message. God gave them the desires of their heart, and He can do it for you as well.

God reminded me, "Keep doing what I say, and you will be fine."

> Romans 12:3 (NIV)
> *"For by the grace given me I say to everyone: Do not think of yourself more highly than you ought, but rather think of yourself with sober judgment, in accordance with the faith God has distributed to each of you."*

For the first time in my life, I am happy with myself. It is hard for me to admit it, but it's true. It took all this time for me to find joy. God showed me my strengths and weaknesses. Sometimes I thought people liked me for what I could give them.

God said, "No. Your humor and character make people comfortable. The anointing I have on your life will always have people drawn to you."

For example, if I see the waitress is having a bad day, I may say, "Come on, come on, just a little bit of a smile for my wife and me." The waitress may give us a little smile, and I would respond with an exciting "Yes! Thank you!"

And she said, "Thank you, Sir."

That simple act of kindness can make a difference in someone else's day. God always puts the right people in your path. So be mindful and look for opportunities to say something to encourage someone else. For example, sometimes, when I am at a gas station. God would show me someone who may not have money to put gas in their car. If it is a lady and my wife is with me, I will ask Debbie to go over and ask if it is okay to bless them by putting more gas in the car.

If God puts it on your heart to bless someone, you should do as He instructs. You do not need permission from anyone else to do what God has called you to do. If anyone ever wants to give you credit, tell them God did it!

WHY YOU WANT TO KNOW ABOUT ME?

The Pandemic

*Obedience is better than sacrifice,
and with obedience comes a reward.*
SHERMAN HARRIS, JR.

In the months preceding the pandemic, God told me to pray for the church and the Body of Christ. God assured me He was going to do something that would impact everyone. He informed me that He was shutting down everything; however, I did not know what it meant.

God said, "You are praying in agreement that I'm going to take care of you and the church while the process is taking place, and you are going to intercede."

God has shown me the blessing of obedience by covering me when I operate in obedience to the Holy Spirit. Obedience is better than sacrifice, and with sacrifice comes a reward. Even amid a global pandemic, God showed me people who would contract COVID-19. Weeks later, I received news of confirmed cases. During the height of the pandemic, God showed me that doctors were not working together for an effective treatment. I heard the lead scientist mention God and the importance of prayer. He was unsure what God was about to do, but he knew God would do something.

I recognized at that time that more doctors needed to have the same faith. I believe twelve of the leading doctors and researchers need to come together in unity to pray to God for a cure. The cure will be so certain that we will never have to wear another mask again. Right now, everyone seems to be about money. It is almost like a hustle. Unity is required for us to move forward beyond the pandemic.

WHY YOU WANT TO KNOW ABOUT ME?

In the Flow

I want to remain in the flow of God.

SHERMAN HARRIS, JR.

I can go anywhere and feel comfortable around anyone, including leading officials in the church. I am reminded of Matthew 13:57 (NIV):

> *And they took offense at him. But Jesus said to them, 'A prophet is not without honor except in his own town and in his own home.'*

God has given me peace and told me, "I don't want you to worry anymore. If I tell you to say something, say it. You have done what I have asked you to do."

I want to remain in the flow of God.

> *"...This kind can come out only by prayer."*
> Mark 9:29 (NIV)

Everyone cannot handle demonic spirits, another level of spiritual warfare. If you are not anointed to handle encounters with demons, do not attempt to lay hands on them. I have seen several demons running toward me while praying for people. The thing I love about God is how He guides me in those encounters. If God instructs me to move in a certain direction, I follow His guidance. For example, God has allowed my wife to assist me in ministering to women with demonic spirits. Sometimes you cannot just pray; fasting is also required. When I fast, I seek God for elevation. Many people fast to lose weight, while others fast for a specific purpose. I seek God for others to receive the messages He has given me to share.

God said, "Let it go."

I do not want anything to hinder me from hearing from God. That will create a blockage, and I will only receive pieces of the message. I want to remain in the flow of God. When a prophet receives pieces, that means they are a false prophet. I will tell you why. They will add their pieces to make the prophetic message clear. The Bible says clearly, do not add or take away anything. There are so many things going on within the church. I don't know what else to do but to allow God to handle the situation.

I know God wants me to start traveling with the Word of God. However, I do not know what else God will do specifically.

I will share why because I asked God the same thing. First Lady Lacey told me years ago, "Don't ever be so humble that you miss your gift." I never understood what she was saying, and now for the first time recently, I understand the meaning.

Sometimes we can be humble. I always say you can never be too humble. You can get humble, and you will mess your gift up. For example, I am invited to many places and turn them down because I don't think I am ready. I am not concerned with fame; I care about

WHY YOU WANT TO KNOW ABOUT ME?

people. I want to speak where and when God leads me. The presence of God will hover; that is where I want to be, in the flow of God. I am not one to run away from my gift. I have known about the prophetic gift for a while. I was not ready then, but I am ready now.

SHERMAN HARRIS, JR

Jealousy

*A heart at peace gives life to the body,
but envy rots the bones.*
PROVERBS 14:30 (NIV)

Whether you know it or not, people are watching you; some are waiting for you to mess up, while others are praying for you to be successful. God has shown me that there are a lot of jealous spirits in the church. I have known this for almost ten years. I don't even know why because jealousy is not justified. Unfortunately, people around you may have a jealous spirit because they feel you should not know what you know.

I began to experience this more recently, confirming a prophecy I received years ago. I warn you of condemning a prophet because a prophecy has not come to pass yet. Isaiah's prophesy was not revealed until 600 years later. Does that mean Isaiah was a false prophet? Not! Everything Isaiah prophesied about Jesus came to pass.

When people only say what they think they know, they are not allowing God to use them. God can uniquely use everyone; there is no need for jealousy in the Kingdom.

WHY YOU WANT TO KNOW ABOUT ME?

I am not trying to imitate or be like anyone else; it will not work because God made each of us for a specific purpose. Even identical twins have different DNA—they do not have the same fingerprints. One day I watched a talk show with Debbie, and one of the guests was the mother of identical twins. The mother shared how it took her six months to recognize the differences in her newborn babies. I told my wife, "I imagine the mother knows the differences in the cries." Shortly after, the mother shared how she differentiated the babies from their cries.

Church people pretend they are not jealous, but I see right through it. We all have unique gifts; therefore, there is no room for jealousy. Our gifts are different, and no one is greater than the other. We are all needed in the Kingdom of God.

Imagine the unity in the church when we operate in our gifts. There will be a Holy Ghost explosion! Our gifts are different but essential to the body of Christ. Your gifts are needed to accomplish the purpose God has for your life. Are you able to utilize your gifts? If we start thinking the way God does, we will realize that God does not always let us have things go our way.

> *"For my thoughts are not your thoughts, neither are your ways my ways, declares the Lord."*
>
> - Isaiah 55:8

SHERMAN HARRIS, JR

Everything In Moderation

Moderation in all things,
Especially moderation.
RALPH WALDO EMERSON

I believe that, as Christians, we cannot put people in a box of perfectionism because no one is perfect. Jesus did not conform to the societal norms of His time; therefore, we should look for creative ways to reach those who do not know Christ. A popular televangelist's wife has ministered to people in strip clubs and street corners over the last nine years. She estimates that over 900 people have accepted Jesus Christ as their Lord and Savior. Talk about out of the box!

My friend Mike recognized the call of God on my life. He told me that since I had changed my life, I could not go to a nightclub or a strip joint. I told him I was on a mission from God. I understand the importance of everything in moderation. I trust that God will not let me fall. I worked with around 66 naked women for seven years and never touched one. God knows my motive is not to go in there to mess around, and He allowed me to go to the clubs to talk to these girls. Each time I visited Atlanta, God allowed me to say something to bless someone.

WHY YOU WANT TO KNOW ABOUT ME?

Mike told me, "Everybody remembers you. The women call you dad, and the guys call you uncle." They appreciated the wisdom and guidance I provided. A young rapper seen on TV called me on my birthday and shared how I changed his life. He doesn't rap anymore because he is a successful real estate investor—he changed his life. He does not fear going to prison anymore for the lifestyle he once lived.

He said, "Man, you changed everything about me." I said, "No, you listened and heard God yourself. That's what happened to you. I just happened to be there for you to listen."

That is why I like God so much! He never puts people in my path without giving me a word to bless, correct, or encourage them. God told me not to worry if the message was not received immediately. Sometimes it may take a while for the people to receive the revelation.

We are programmed to go through the motions regarding prayer and service to others. The question to ponder is, "Are we truly seeking God?" God told us to seek His kingdom first, and His righteousness and everything else will be added. There is a time and season for everything. We must be careful, even praying. Some people ask for prayer for specific things and areas, but I do not want people I pray for to feel they have to tell me. The Spirit reveals the need to me.

I will not go against God's will, so whatever God's will be, that is what I pray. I believe in praying for families to be strengthened; therefore, I pray for families to receive peace, joy, happiness, and understanding. God is still blessing us. Regardless of whatever God decides to do, we are still blessed. If we are still here, there is still more to do in Jesus' name. I am at peace with His will.

SHERMAN HARRIS, JR

Get Rid of Fear and Trust God

*The trust level we think we have
differs from what we have.*
SHERMAN HARRIS, JR.

I am not afraid of anyone but God. In the streets, I was The Man, and people respected me. I respect my pastor, and if I am honest, I wanted to please him. I asked God why I felt that desire. God said, "You always want to do that with authority. I watched you when you worked at Target."

Besides hustling and running my business, Target is the only job I have ever worked, aside from my volunteer work as a coach. Coaching never felt like a job. I had to be on time at Target, reporting to work at 8:00 a.m. I remained punctual. I learned the importance of being submissive, even to my manager. Whenever they said to do something, I would comply to the best of my ability. I believed in submitting to authority.

God told me to work there for one and a half years, and I did to the day. I put my two weeks' notice in and everything. I take a day off for my entire period of employment. My whole life changed after I left Target.

WHY YOU WANT TO KNOW ABOUT ME?

There were things done in the past that I did not go along with in the church. I asked God, "Why don't you help me?"

God showed me. I will never forget, He said, "I need you to be his protector. It is because you will tell the truth. You will be honest." For some reason, he wouldn't heed my counsel. Was it because, at the time, I did not have a title? God told me I was available and obedient, qualities he needed most. It took the pandemic, but finally, my pastor is listening.

God questioned me, "Why would I give you something to say that will disrespect the pastor? I know you love him."

"Who will you please, man or God?" Galatians 1:10.

Am I trying to win the approval of God, or am I trying to please people? If I were still trying to please people, I would not be a servant of Christ.

I cannot wait for God to take the roof off the church. Seeing Him move miraculously within the church and the body of Christ (believers of Christ) is amazing. The growth will occur when we align with God and everyone is in the proper position, using their spiritual gifts.

We will see a remarkable change if we are obedient and listen to God's words. This will happen not because I have The Word to give but because God is ready to do it. Then, there will be a release within the church. I want us to know the difference between when God says it happens or not. God is ready to release the church, and I pray it is received because prophecy will come to pass if you believe it. On the contrary, prophecy will not come to pass if you do not think it will happen.

If you doubt it, do not do it. If you twist it to fit your liking, it will not come to pass. If God says to do "ABC" and you go and do "DEFG," it will not work. It is just that simple.

Get rid of fear and trust God. Your experiences will blow your mind. Continue to pray for our pastors and leaders. We must pray and fast for their wisdom. Be sure to surround yourself with people who will always tell you the truth without being a "yes" person. We need honesty, so get rid of fear and trust God.

I enjoy going to seminars with other like-minded men. My pastoral friends attended a conference with me at the D.C. Convention Center. I learned so much during our time together. Leaving the event, I said, "Look how much I am learning around these giants in the ministry." I call them giants because they are doing great work, and I learn so much from them. It may sound crazy, but if I'm trying to understand something better, I must surround myself with the right people.

God told me, "I like your attitude, but what makes you think they know more than you?"

He said, "Who do you think is speaking to you?"

I said, "You!"

He said, "How do they know more than you?"

I said, "God, you know these people are sharper than me."

He said, "Who talks to you?"

I said, "You do."

He said, "So they are smarter than me? I want you to keep this in mind: I do not mind you listening and learning, but they are not smarter than me."

God rebukes me often. The truth is required in this season. I will not tell a watered-down truth. Do you realize how powerful the truth is? You may be mad the first time someone tells you the truth. But eventually, happiness will come when we recognize the freedom it brings.

WHY YOU WANT TO KNOW ABOUT ME?

Our kids need the truth. I guarantee the next generation will accept the truth better than we did. Imagine a child feeling: I *can trust my parents*.

That's what the truth does. If we start with lies and then shift to truths, we confuse the kids (and ourselves.) God is not the author of confusion.

John 8:32 states:
"And ye shall know the truth, and the truth shall make you free."

SHERMAN HARRIS, JR

God Is in Control

*For my thoughts are not your thoughts,
neither are your ways my ways,
declares the Lord.*
ISAIAH 55:8-9

God gave us free will. Free will is the ability to make decisions based on one's choice. I always thought that God could never be in control of something evil. Take, for example, killing someone. How can God be in control of someone killing another human being? The act goes against everything God embodies. For this reason, I believe God is not in control.

I talked about this concept in 2008 at Pastor Davis' church. Then, when I did more study on God's ways, I told them that I recognized that God is in control. But first, I will tell you why I had to change my perspective on why I thought God was not in control.

Recently, God gave me something to help me see things differently. I know God is never in confusion. As a human being, I oversee my thoughts and actions, but I am not always in control. We have all heard of someone losing control of their emotions.

God showed me that He is both in charge and in control. He does not stop people from losing control because He has given us free

WHY YOU WANT TO KNOW ABOUT ME?

will. Not because He does not have control. By giving humanity free will, He allows us to make choices, but He is still in control. I had to apologize since I learned differently. However, God gave me a reason to explain the growth. He is in control because He gave you free will.

When someone lacks self-control, there is often evidence of impulsive, reactive behaviors, sometimes even extreme behaviors such as stabbing or shooting someone. Usually, that individual is reacting based on emotions such as anger. I thought about that for a long time. How can you think that God is in control of you, imposing harm on someone? That is the flesh. God can stop it, but He does not go against our free will. We can make good choices, or we can make bad choices.

Even when we make bad choices, God still loves us. Think about that. That is enough to jump up and down with gratitude. I think about all the stuff I have done outside of His will. I only sometimes did what was right. I thank God for His grace. I thank God for His amazing grace!

Recently I was at church one Sunday. The Holy Spirit showed me some things to help the church that would have demonstrated the message, but I did not feel the church was ready to receive the message.

I must please God. I can't worry about what anyone thinks of me. Deep down in my heart, I want others to be pleased with me, but I am okay if they are never pleased with me if I please God. I must do what God has called me to do. I must give it the way God gave me to deliver and let it be. God is not amid confusion. God would not give me a word to sow discord.

The key is to have a listening ear. If you are angry or frustrated, these emotions do not mix with hearing from God. Allow me to explain. If you are angry or frustrated and praying, you will only hear yourself. I'll say it again. You can think you are hearing from God, but God is not a part of that. Can you imagine being in God's presence? I get chills now just thinking about it. Yet, these are the things God allows me to see.

Suppose someone comes to deliver a message that destroys you by speaking down or embarrassing you. That is not a prophet. God does not destroy you. God blesses you. God corrects us so we can be blessed (Hebrews 12:6). He loves us so much that He corrects us when we go astray. For me, it's a blessing. I love when He checks me. With each rebuke, He takes me to the next level. If I keep thinking I know everything, I will never learn anything.

When I do not prophesy as I should, God corrects me. God says, "You did it again. You delivered pieces of it. You did not do all of it."

Honestly, I thought it would be too much. But, when I think about it now, I recognize that God purposed me to be in that space in time to deliver His message. God told me to sit there. I did that part right. One of the pastors asked me what was wrong, and I informed him, "God told me to sit here."

He said, "Okay. So that must mean you are saying something today if God has you sitting here."

Sure enough, God did, but I did not do everything. It was out of respect for the leadership. I wanted to stay within my boundaries. I do not believe God will punish me for growing in this process.

It is okay to be loyal, but we cannot be so loyal that we do not have any say. Loyalty is not saying yes to everything someone says or does. That is a dictatorship. There is a difference. There is a time to speak up. God has given me the wisdom and knowledge to know when and how to speak. I call it laying it down in a good, comfortable way. As leaders, we cannot think our way is the only way. What God is telling you, do not put anything with it.

One of my buddies told me that people from the neighborhood remembered how I was running the streets and hustling. So, now I am traveling across the nation ministering the Word of God, prophesying over people's lives, and it comes to pass. He asked if I was willing to expose everything in this book. Yes, here you have it all. Everything, from selling drugs to womanizing. Not to glamorize any of it but to show how God transformed my life. So, my friend asked if I was willing to expose myself. So, whatever you want to call it, here it is.

He said, "If God can take you from there to a prophet. I believe it was there all the time."

He protected me. I am trying to understand why I never got locked up. People asked me if I would snitch. I do not know because I was never busted. I get that question all the time. I honestly do not know if I would have snitched. I may have told on someone. I would not want to be one, but I will never know.

I'm so grateful, though, I'll tell you. I'm so blessed. I am not talking about money. I want to make that clear. Right now, I have 14 people on staff, and I don't have enough workers to complete the work.

I have learned it now, and it's just beautiful; especially when I see strangers accepting what God is doing through me. It means a lot. I was in Walmart one day, and a lady was trying to pay for her groceries with a bag full of change. I slid enough money to the cashier to cover the groceries and asked her to give the change to the customer. I gave the money and walked out. The customer was so happy that she yelled, "Thank you." It blessed me to see a smile on her face. I just waved at her. I love being at the right place at the right time.

WHY YOU WANT TO KNOW ABOUT ME?

Blessings On Blessings

Give, and it will be given to you.
A good measure, pressed down,
shaken together, and running over,
will be poured into your lap.
For with the measure you use,
it will be measured to you.
Luke 6:38

I frequent several restaurants with my friends and family. My favorite restaurants are Antonio's, The Family Restaurant, Silverado's, Spartans, Texas Roadhouse, and IHOP. I visited IHOP twice a week before the pandemic, but now it is usually once a week. I enjoy leaving large tips to bless the wait staff for their hard work. One of my buddies noticed and asked if I bless them every time, I frequent the restaurant. I told him yes.

I told him that God put me in a position to help others, and I am addicted to giving. As a result, servers always take care of us and provide the best customer service. Anyone with me is treated the same way. The servers lavish Debbie with gifts like tennis shoes and other little gifts to show appreciation.

I am blessed and thankful to be a blessing to others. I pray to one day go into communities, not just during Thanksgiving and Christmas, and bless entire communities by providing free repairs to their homes. I would love to remodel their homes at no cost to them, covering supplies, materials, and labor. I want to encourage others to take pride in their homes by keeping them clean, and in return, I would provide necessities such as clothing and groceries. That is my prayer.

One of my mentees, Shivon, partnered with me to bless families with gift cards. I allowed the Holy Spirit to lead me to different retailers to give. I have a special place in my heart for families with multiple children. We want the best for people, that is all. I do not know why God sent me to Walmart, but that is where he sent me. I pray the recipients felt the love of God when they received the blessing.

WHY YOU WANT TO KNOW ABOUT ME?

Driven

Be driven with purpose.

DR. STEVE MARABOLI

For many years, I was driven in my car by others. Today, I drive myself, and God downloads a lot to me. Recently God told me while working on this book, "Whatever I give you for that day is what you will share. There may be some days when I may stay on certain subjects. Do not force this process."

I want to be closer to God, so I worship Him daily with songs of praise and worship continually. God carries me when I'm riding down the highway. I enjoy listening to scriptures from the Bible while commuting to worksites. When I am in the presence of God, I do not want to leave. I recall times when I made it to my destination and had no recollection of the drive, only my time with God.

I was so deep in the presence of God that I heard a woman blow her horn at me. It was as if she knew I was in deep meditation. When I opened my eyes, the voice said, "I got you." So now, there are times when I do not put on certain worship music. God leads me in the songs I select.

I know we must come out of our worship. There are times early in the morning when I can't sleep, and God begins to speak to me, usually around 3 a.m., and keeps me up for an hour. Once I lay back down, I am usually back up at 6 a.m. I have my first phone call with the guys. I talk to people daily, throughout the day, at different times. I enjoy speaking to them, praying with them, and encouraging them. I told them I thank God for them because they have been my Bible. We go through the scriptures together. We hold one another accountable.

A friend from Charlotte, North Carolina, asked me how I knew what scriptures to go to when driving on the highway. She asked me if I had the verses memorized. I told her I did not know what the scriptures I shared said. People laugh when they hear this, but Shivon can tell you I do not read it first to see what is in it. I give what God tells me to give. It's just what they need right then and there. I have never thought about I said no, I know.

God told me, "*Why you want to know about me*" is for a purpose. So, I said, "OK, God, I'm good." I want people to see that God is real. You may not know me. But I want you to know that God is allowing you to get to know who I am and, most importantly, what He has done to change my life, and most importantly, He can also transform my life.

I do not know what God is going to do. I think I'm there to sign a book. But God may have me there for another purpose. God has a purpose specifically for you. The Gospel songwriter penned a true statement: "what God has for me; it is for me." No demon can stop it. I will tell you something better: You cannot stop it. I love God. His purpose for your life cannot be stopped. His will is going to be done. Please make no mistake about it.

God's will, will be done.

WHY YOU WANT TO KNOW ABOUT ME?

Someone wanted to do a documentary on me in DC in 1995. They only wanted to showcase the gangster and hustler lifestyle. Even then, I did not want to spotlight this aspect of my life. The directors were impressed that none of my people got busted while I was in the game. No one was ever killed. I stressed about making money and not killing. They wanted to convey that part and show others how I handled business.

The director also appreciated the way I talked to women, especially the ones that were prostituting. They could get off the streets by becoming performers at the club. They were able to make their own money without the pimps beating them. I bought a house off Rhode Island Ave for them to live in, and they paid me rent. I had two guys to serve as security to protect them if someone tried to harm them. No prostitution was allowed. They were exotic dancers, and they made their own money. What they did after hours was their business. But there was no one going to beat them and take their money.

I want to make sure that people hear this. Men have certain attractions. I don't care who you are—preacher, prophet, or apostle—your position does not matter. If that temptation confronts you, what will you do? I cannot speak for anyone else when that attraction comes to or around me. I state to myself, "My wife is my everything. Devil, you will not tempt me today. I'm going home to my wife. I am not even walking over there." I'm not even speaking. I do not even want to put myself in that position.

Debbie asked me, "Why did you turn to go there?"

I said, "Debbie did you see that attractive woman up there? She reminded me of you when I first became attracted to you. I'm not going up there."

She said, "I am not worried."

I said, "I know you're not worried about it, but I am not even going to put myself in that position where I must get back in the car. I am married, so I'm gone."

As men, we can become cocky and think we cannot succumb to temptation. Everyone has some temptations. I never wanted to be caught being a junkie or drug addict, so I never messed with it. I never had to worry about getting caught doing drugs. That was my philosophy. I was determined not to do drugs. I did have a habit. I liked to gamble. There is no difference in addictive behaviors—people like what they like.

My wife and I laugh when we see a guy on television with a nice build. I tell her I am not built like that. I'm not stupid. I know that my wife likes a man with muscles. The same is true for someone who likes cars. For every car you like, you cannot buy it or even drive it. We like it, but we do not buy it. I know my wife likes the muscles for a reason. That does not mean that she does not love me. I understand that. I do not think she is in love with every built man with muscles.

I love how she compliments other women. So many women will not do that. She is a very genuine person. She even compliments men when they are dressed nicely. She finds a way to encourage and compliment others, one of many things I love about her.

We were in a store once, and this lady walked up to her and complimented her. Everywhere we go, someone stops her and compliments her. I don't care if she is wearing a pair of jeans and going to Walmart or stopping to eat at a restaurant. Somebody always manages to stop us and compliment her.

One man said, "Don't get mad at me, but she looks so good."

I said, "I would be mad if you didn't say it."

WHY YOU WANT TO KNOW ABOUT ME?

If a man doesn't want his wife to look good, something is wrong with him. You better want your wife looking good. It is a great feeling to grow together, spend time, create memories, and laugh together. We love looking at television and movies together.

The move of God has gotten my attention. I asked God why he would take a risk with me. I ask God often, "Why would you gamble with me? Why would you trust me enough with these words and these powerful gifts, allowing me to see things down the road? Showing me things and visions."

God said, "I am putting you in a position to see things in the Spirit. So, therefore, do not be afraid of the things you see."

I have read Deuteronomy, and Isaiah 43:1-10 reminds me not to be afraid. God has me. I have a heart for the people and deliver God's message to correct and bless. Every correction is not bad. Correction is God finding the way to bless us. Suppose we don't understand this principle. We will struggle with it. That is why many people cannot take correction. The truth is the only way. So why do we need help with hearing the truth?

SHERMAN HARRIS, JR

Worthy

*I'm not deserving,
but I'm worthy,
because I'm called.*
SHERMAN HARRIS, JR.

All my life, I have been taught that I am not worthy. So, one day, while reading, I thought about looking up the word worthy. But I decided against it because why would God take the time to create someone in His image who is not worthy?

You do not have to know the definition to know that you are worthy because God made you! If you are going to say anything, say we do not deserve God's grace and mercy. Reflecting on my life, I accept that I do not deserve God's grace. As I look at my life, I do not deserve all His blessings, but do not tell me I am not worthy because He created me to be worthy; therefore, I am worthy!

God positions me to see things and reminds me, "I told you when you share a prophetic message, you will see some things. I send you there for a purpose—to help them and bless them. Nobody is perfect. You are not perfect. That is what I love about you. Always tell people it is not you but Me."

WHY YOU WANT TO KNOW ABOUT ME?

Drop the Ball

> You can drop it,
> but it never breaks.
> SHERMAN HARRIS, JR.

Despite all my faults, I always tell my wife how grateful I am to God for covering us. I believe God gave me that message because many men understand sports. I asked God what He would have for me to share with women since He has given me so much for the guys.

God said to call this chapter 'drop the ball.' Anyone can drop something. God said to let women know that they can never be broken. Even if you fall or if you drop something, it never breaks. God hands the ball back when it is dropped, which is way better than when you first received it. Way better!

During one of the *Iron Sharpens Iron* Monday morning calls, I told the guys we were on the goal line. It was first, and goal to go, and I dropped the ball. I fumbled and messed up again. God picked up the ball and handed it back to me. The next play, I dropped the ball again, and He picked it up and handed it right back to me. Now it is third down in football. I drop it again. He hands it right back to me. Now it is fourth down and we go for it, touchdown!

Sometimes it takes us a few times to get to the goal. But we still got there. The jealousy comes in when one player gets it on the first run. He wants to compare himself to the one who took four downs to score. The points are the same. As people, we judge one another. We look at how we are gifted to do things, in this case, score on the first run. The player who made the play on the first run will be sure to tell the other player it took him four downs. They both scored six points. It does not matter how many times it takes.

God showed me the same thing when it comes to someone who is a great reader. I'm looking for people that can read well. God said, "Don't you know someone out there who can out-read her?" I love to have Shivon read to me. I'm comfortable with her reading certain things to me. I get a revelation when she reads things to me. I get blessed every time she reads to me. Our relationship has continued to blossom over the years.

Each of the young ladies that I mentored over the years has special gifts. Tiesha helped me understand the people that are calling me for prayer. Specifically, to see if God has revealed something to me. I'm struggling with it because these people do not normally call. Suppose it was somebody that normally calls me. I'm okay with it. I have enough discernment to know this person would like me to give them a word from God. Tiesha said I should not look at it that way. She suggests that maybe God is using them to call me. I know they hardly speak to you. But do you think God might use them to reach out to you?

If God does not give you anything for them, there is nothing to give. But do not get an attitude when there is nothing from God. God turned my perspective on this situation when He told me, "You use me. There are many times when you do not do what I told you to do. But you came back to me."

WHY YOU WANT TO KNOW ABOUT ME?

I said, "God, okay. You are right."

If a prophet cannot be taught, he is not a prophet. If I begin to think that because God talks to me and no one else can talk to me, but what God, something is wrong with me.

God uses everybody in a way. Even the bad, He will turn it into good. It should not matter whom God uses; it is our responsibility to receive the things God must deliver. The primary principle is to learn to take responsibility and be open to reality. God can turn any situation, not tomorrow, but now!

SHERMAN HARRIS, JR

Handle Your Anger

*"Anger doesn't solve anything.
It builds nothing,
but it can destroy everything."*
LAWRENCE DOUGLAS WILDER

I don't care how old you are; you cannot make a good decision when you are angry. I don't think any human being can make a great, responsible decision when angry or frustrated. God is not in confusion.

When you are angry, you cannot think clearly. It may seem as if you are not yourself. You split from your normal persona. I call it a split personality, not in the mental sense, but as an emotional response. I have never seen an angry person make a good decision. How often have we said or done something to someone in our family? Then, after stepping away for a minute, we think, man, I should not have said or done that.

I say, "God, you have not told me to say any of that."

We are all prone to respond out of frustration or anger. After the anger has subsided, you must call the person back, apologize and ask God for forgiveness.

WHY YOU WANT TO KNOW ABOUT ME?

We go to God and ask Him questions. I call these moments "conversations with God." Sometimes we may feel that God is not responding. But, if you feel you are close to an answer, then you are. Anytime you are willing to go 50/50 with God, that is you and God; then you are there. If you have a relationship with God and the Holy Spirit has assured you, then you have your answer.

Whatever you do, God will protect you. There is no wrong answer. Just say it. What happens is we sit back and keep waiting. He has already told you to proceed. What stops you from moving forward is your anger—your frustration. We get frustrated when God does not respond how we feel He should. Or God does not respond as quickly as we would like Him to respond. Now we cannot hear from God. He has responded. Now the cycle starts over again. God has answered, but we missed it. Trust God enough to let it be.

I am reminded of Psalm 34 when David pretended to be insane with Abimelech. Like David, I pretended. I pretended, and God protected me. I was none of the things people thought I was. I never shot a gun, and people thought I was a killer. My façade was my defense mechanism for dealing with the bullying and name-calling I endured during school. I had to defend myself.

I see it play out in our society today when I see other people trying to be someone they are not. If we were to visit jail and talk to someone sentenced to 50 years or more, they would make a different choice if they could go back and stop and think for 30 seconds. Not thinking can change your entire life. Get control of your anger.

SHERMAN HARRIS, JR

Honor Your Word

*Your word is your honor.
If you say you're going
to do something,
you need to do it.*
JOYCE MEYER

Have you ever told someone you would pray for them and didn't? Sometimes it is best to pray for them right then and there because life gets busy, and you may forget. So, try to be a man or woman of your word. But we must watch our words.

I used to love listening to gossip, and I considered it to be information sharing or conversations about other people, but not anymore. I immediately shut it down when someone calls me and starts with something negative about someone else. I do not want it in my house. My wife and I have never had problems in our household for over 22 years. If we start bringing negativity into our homes, problems will appear. I'm trying to do what I can to address problems before they show up.

We will not let the devil ease into our home through gossip. I do not want that; although I used to love gossip—I was king of it. I loved hearing the stories and details because I thought it was information. That is not information. Let's say you have a good friend. You and this friend get along very well, but then someone else comes along and tells you something negative about your friend. Imagine hearing negativity about your friend. You may begin to start seeing your friend in a different light. Be careful with what you allow to enter your spirit through gossip.

I don't care. If a seed of negativity is planted, it will grow. Good or bad, it will be revealed. I am not a farmer, but every seed planted is not good. Weeds grow automatically. I am not talking about holiness. This has to do with principles. As people, we must learn the importance of our words.

People say, "I made a mistake and cursed." How is cursing a mistake? I'm not going to call cursing a mistake. Is profanity the best terminology to use? No. Say what you have to say. Let that thing go because it will do more damage to your body while holding it inside. We have gotten so holy that we cannot speak our truth.

All things work together for the good of those who love God. Everything is good, and even that bad is good because it takes us to another level. If we continue to do things our way, in the flesh, we will remain in that section when we become accustomed to doing things our way. Using profanity or speaking our minds is staying in that section.

Why do we feel so comfortable doing and saying what we want? I do not want to feel comfortable doing wrong. Rebuke me when I am wrong. Although I know I am not perfect and will do wrong, do not let me enjoy doing wrong. We are not going to do everything right. I do not call it a mistake. Let that thing go and ask God for forgiveness. Honor your word. If you say you are going to do something, do it. Honoring your word is a basic premise we honor. Our youth are watching us whether we know it or not.

The youth are the church's future, so we should bring the kids back to the church, and we can do it without tricks. I want to talk to the youth about their gifts. It is important for youth not to be ashamed of their gifts. Let your gifts do what they do. Do not let anyone say anything that will take away your confidence. You can do it because God gave it to you. It is our responsibility to equip our youth. It is our responsibility to encourage our youth. I understand the importance of doing what we can because I had self-esteem issues growing up.

I found out a lot about myself during a recent sabbatical. The top thing I learned was the fear and low self-esteem issues I had. I did not believe I could do what God wanted me to do. It is almost like I was going along with it. If I am honest, I did not believe in my ability to be used by God. Yet, for years I thought I had this great discerning spirit.

During the sabbatical, God began to tell me things about myself. First, he showed me I was uncomfortable using my gift because my reading and speaking skills made me feel I was not qualified to do what I needed for God. It had nothing to do with my abilities.

God told me, "You don't need anything to repeat what I say to you." When He told me this, it reminded me that when I was in the streets, I always thought I had to be a touch-off guy. I always thought I had to have money or play the role of a tough guy because women like tough guys. Women like hustlers, so I thought I had to play those roles. When I look back over my life, I never wanted to hustle.

WHY YOU WANT TO KNOW ABOUT ME?

God Knows

*Before I formed you in the womb, I knew you,
before you were born, I set you apart;
I appointed you as a prophet to the nations.*

JEREMIAH 1:5

We must learn to take responsibility and admit our shortcomings. Accept responsibility for the bad choice. In the process, talk to yourself about how you messed up. Review ways to improve and ask God to help you improve.

I told God one day around 4:00 p.m. I said, "God, I do not want to mess up tomorrow like I did today."

God asked me to repeat what I said, and I did. He said, "It is 4:00 p.m. Are you telling me you want to stay like this for the rest of the day?"

I was talking about tomorrow, and the day was not even over. We have the power to shift our current state. We must know the power we possess. This self-awareness comes from learning to take responsibility. We have more power than we think.

Even when hustling, God protected me because I never went to jail. I know God knew what He had for me to do. As I look back, I say God knew. He recognized that I would do what He needed me to do. I did not know it, but God knew. God knew I could help many people, but I had to start with myself. He saved me for a time like this.

When a prophet says something to a person, the person must have the right motive. This is because the prophecy will only be received if the motive is right when the prophet speaks. Not that the prophecy is wrong, but the individual may not be able to receive it.

I asked, "God, why would you let me say it to them?" He said, "because you have to say it. You must release it." When you talk to that person, and somebody else is there, they might get it. The intended person may have missed it, but another person may get it. When a prophet speaks out loud to people, the person you want to receive it might not get it, but somebody else who needed to hear it got what they needed.

My responsibility as a prophet is to release the message. So, when God told me to say something, I figured the person automatically received it. I may have been ignorant, but I always thought that when He said something to me that the person got understanding when it was prophesied.

I told God I understood and asked Him, "Why do they not understand what you are saying to them?"

It was revealed to me that it comes down to free will. God will not take free will away.

God told me, "I tell you this, once you say what I say, they'll receive it down the road. Down the road, they'll see it. In so many words, they will get it."

Romans 14:11 says every knee will bow. That is God's word. Not ours. I wonder about atheists and those who do not trust or don't believe. Those who do not believe in God. Will they ever trust God?

WHY YOU WANT TO KNOW ABOUT ME?

I asked myself that many times. I understand Christians, but you tell me every knee will bow. Every means everybody; everyone will confess Jesus as Lord.

SHERMAN HARRIS, JR

Just Like He Said

*For promotion cometh neither from the east,
nor from the west, nor from the south.
But God is the judge: he putteth down one,
and setteth up another.*
PSALM 75:6-7(KJV)

One of the young ladies I mentor called me frustrated about not getting promoted because the selected individual was less qualified. I assured her that God was designing a job specifically for her. I encouraged her to be patient and informed her that a man would call her soon for a position that would blow her mind.

A few weeks later, she called me screaming. She reminded me of what I said. Then, finally, she exclaimed, "You know what you said a few weeks ago?"

I assured her, "I know what *He* said."

She said, "Well, He has done it."

She was thrilled to be able to bless her mother and accomplish some things she wanted to achieve professionally.

I asked her, "How did it happen?"

Her response was, "Just like you said."

WHY YOU WANT TO KNOW ABOUT ME?

I asked her, "Who?"

She said, "Just like *He* said."

There is no way I could know what and how things would transpire in the lives of the people of God. God gets the glory in every situation. I am no crystal ball, and I trust God enough to say what He tells me to say. That is the key. A key I learned the hard way.

Once, a young lady kept pressing me for scripture. I was driving down the road, and she would not let me get off the phone until I gave her a scripture. Notice what I said. *I* gave her a scripture. But that scripture was so off base.

God reminded me, "See what kind of scriptures you give versus what I give." All I could do was laugh. He instantly showed me my word versus His word.

This was not the first time God showed me the importance of His word versus mine. I repeated something I heard a popular televangelist share during a conference I attended a few weeks before this encounter. The room was filled with about 40 attendees. Immediately after I repeated what I had heard at the previous conference, a couple of guys raised their hands and asked me to break down what I shared in a way they could understand.

I was embarrassed, and I had to come clean. I told the men I did not know what my statement meant, but I was confident the Holy Spirit would reveal the meaning before I left the conference. I told them I appreciated them for asking the question because I would only repeat something I heard if I fully understood.

I learned my lesson. Just because I heard another anointed vessel deliver the word did not mean I should repeat it without revelation. Before the conference ended, the Holy Spirit led me to share from Hebrews, and we had a good time sharing from the Word of God.

God said, "I protected you that time. Do not do it again. I do not care who is preaching. Study it for yourself, then you can repeat it. Study first. Then repeat." I still wonder why God would put me in a position and talk to these people. Why would God use me? That is why I always say fools and babes. God trusts me enough to tell others what he says.

I can't lie to God because He knows. There is no way I can tell God I don't sometimes think when He tells me things. I do, but I tell it anyway because I know His voice. I have a relationship with him and know when He speaks to me. I do not always fully understand what I am told to share, but I trust Him. I will honor the word He gives me to speak. We all have a gift. We should be grateful, thankful, and growing until we leave this earth. When growing stops, we are dead anyway.

When I go places, the moment I start speaking, I'm speaking what God gives me. That's it. Nothing more. Nothing less. We keep saying we want to see something new, but when God shows up unexpectedly, we have a problem. How do you want something new but cannot accept it when it shows up?

In 2006, God anointed my voice to speak and pray. Others have noticed it as well. Someone once said I pray with prophecy. I asked, "What do you mean?"

She said that most of the time when I pray, I begin with a prophecy then I pray for the people. So, I talked to God about the comments, and God assured me, "I'm telling you what to say, so how can there be any confusion? Do not lose your confidence."

I do not realize what I am doing—I just want to do what God says. Because of my growth journey, I do not want to do anything without God. I don't want anyone to think that I'm saying these things or that I'm guessing or don't fully comprehend a concept.

WHY YOU WANT TO KNOW ABOUT ME?

One Sunday, God told me to stay put after service. God led me to speak over one of the youths of the church. The father came up to me and said everything I said was right.

I said, "No, don't make it about me. Everything *God* says is right. I know nothing about your family, and I know nothing about your son. God is doing that. He is just using me."

That is the best way for me to operate. I am so happy to watch God move. I told the shy young man not to fall for the peer pressure he was facing. I told him, "You do not want to go along with them, so they call you lame. So let them call you lame. Do not worry about it."

I told him he would have a different set of friends, and the people he was with then would not be his friends later. So, to any youth or parent of a child facing a challenge, have enough patience. Keep being what you say, and watch what God does in your life and the lives of those around you.

SHERMAN HARRIS, JR

You Are the One

God will never put you in a position of regret.

SHERMAN HARRIS, JR.

I was invited to speak at an outdoor conference. There were over 200 people in attendance. I walked past a lady with an oxygen tank, and God told me to pray for her. I told God I did not know her, and He pointed out I did not know anyone there. I was guided to the front of the crowd. As I began to speak, I began to share a prophetic message. God instructed me to tell the lady with the oxygen tank to take three deep breaths, and she would not need the tank anymore.

I said, "God, I cannot do that." I was thinking of the risks. What if the lady died? I continued, "God, I hear you, but I cannot do that. If she does not breathe, it is like I'm killing her."

God said, "Do you think I would have you kill that lady?" I was still paralyzed by fear. My friend Chris approached me and said, "That lady with the oxygen tank over there is staring at you."

I walked toward her, and she said, "You are the one who has something to say to me." I was astonished to see God at work. God

WHY YOU WANT TO KNOW ABOUT ME?

said to me, "Do you think I would have you cause harm to her? You heard what I said."

I did as God instructed. I told the lady to take breaths, and she did, and I was at peace. I was in the community a few weeks after this encounter. A lady approached me and asked me if I knew who she was. I informed her I did not know her. She said, "I am the lady with the oxygen tank. Look at me now."

I just shook my head. God did just as He said! That was my first known encounter with God. It was in Alexandria. God was with me all along. I thought it was a discerning spirit because I did not know anything about the gift of prophecy.

The voice would tell me not to go to certain places, and I did not go. I learned to listen, even when I did not understand why I was led to do something. I always thought I was lucky. I never saw myself preaching, praying, and prophesying at a church.

During my early years, I attended small conferences and started a fellowship called "Snatch the Man." I was being obedient to what God called me to do. My bishop recently said he saw my gift when I first started attending church. Honestly, I did not believe him. I told him how I truly felt.

He explained that he wanted me to recognize God's call on my life. All the previous churches I attended wanted me to be a preacher, so I left. My bishop explained that he was concerned about asking me to serve as a deacon because he thought I would leave. He was right because I always left when approached about serving as a minister. He knew something was different about me, and he was right. I eased out. I never wanted to be a pastor or a preacher.

I attended a men's conference several years ago. There were over 600 men in attendance. I was the second person to receive a prophetic message.

The prophet said to me, "Oh my God. You are the one with the gift. Not only that, but you will also speak in multiple tongues. Your tongues are going to get you in many places."

I asked myself, "What is wrong with this man?"

He continued, "People already fear you. You see things. Can you share with this congregation what God is telling you right now? I will give you the mic. You know something about me right now."

I whispered to him what God gave me to share, addressing his personal struggle.

He took the mic and said, "He is gifted," as he passed the microphone to another bishop, he hugged me and thanked me for not exposing him. God will never put you in a position of regret.

WHY YOU WANT TO KNOW ABOUT ME?

Fear Had to Be Checked

Everything you want is on the other side of fear.

JACK CANFIELD

I thought my concern about the opinion of others regarding my gift was out of respect, and I later learned it was fear. Why are we mad at the enemy when he is simply doing his job? That is misplaced anger; we should be mad at ourselves for believing his tactics. I will make it personal. I should never let anyone affect me negatively. I have been in the streets with gangsters and never experienced fear.

I've always respected leaders. My father and my mother raised me that way. I respect leaders, and I believe it should be reciprocated. If I feel like I have been mishandled, I will address the issue right away in a respectful manner. I will say what I have to say and walk away. I do not believe in arguments and going back and forth to prove a point. I do not want to live with regrets or sorrow, so I will make my point and walk away; otherwise, there may be some trouble. If you are in a confrontational situation, I encourage you to walk away until you can calm down.

I am learning not to sugarcoat what God has given me to share. As a result, I'm able to be direct with almost everyone. I say almost everyone because I had much fear I did not recognize until God revealed it to me during a sabbatical. I am grateful God showed me how to handle the fear that paralyzed me from doing what God called me to do.

I had to take control of my destiny. It is easy to blame everyone else, but I had to be honest with myself. It came down to my low self-esteem. I realized my insecurities manifested when it was time to operate in my gift. My inability to operate effectively made me seek God for direction, and He gave me the confidence and clarity I needed.

We misplace blame with others when we should take ownership of ourselves. Placing blame in the right place requires us to look ourselves in the mirror. Try it. Look at your reflection. How many pimples do you have? Pimples in this analogy represent our problems, and our blemishes represent our issues. Take a closer look. We all have imperfections.

We think life is easy because we love God. However, even with a relationship with God, we will have problems. No one is exempt; even the trailblazers in the ministry have unspoken challenges and issues they have not shared with anyone. God has given me a message for several leaders in the faith community. When we meet, I will share what God has given me. They will know the message is from God because He has them on a mission. Believe it or not, you are on a mission as well.

Once you are on a mission with God, He elevates you to a different level. Imagine the unity when thousands of people worldwide can come together to fast and pray. Fasting and prayer prepare us for the movement of God and when God moves, be careful not to become

WHY YOU WANT TO KNOW ABOUT ME?

too prideful, but you will have to acknowledge there are only some things God can do.

I feel spoiled by God. He takes such good care of me. I do not study as much as I used to, and I feel like I am using God. I do not want to hear about what I did many years ago when I stayed in the basement, learning, and growing in God. So many of my friends in ministry remind me that I should not feel the way I feel. I cannot live on the Word from many years ago. That is why I fast, pray, and take sabbaticals. I want to get back in the room with God.

My worship has me thinking differently. Things that once upset me no longer upset me. Certain situations do not intimidate me anymore. I can leave it and let it go. That is because of the grace and mercy of God. I used to worry about what people thought about me. I beat that, but now I have another problem. God told me this would happen until I met him.

I got rid of my fear of trying to please people, and God informed me that another fear was around the corner. We will always fear something. The flesh finds something to fear or worry about. The only thing we should fear is God.

SHERMAN HARRIS, JR

If Anyone Asks

They will know about God when I finish –
How God turned my life around.
SHERMAN HARRIS, JR.

If anyone asks me how I want to be remembered; I pray God is pleased with how I told the truth in the end due to the changes He made in my life. I pray I did something positive for God and helped His people. That is what I want to be known as, a man who pleased God. I want to hear Him say, "Well done, thy good and faithful servant." I live each day to accomplish His purpose for my life. When I wake up, I say, "Forgive me for every thought I have now and every thought I will think of later. I repent right now if it is not of you."

I recognize thoughts and past experiences ambush me as a distraction from the purpose and plan of God. Someone once asked me how I went from having millions of dollars to nothing without going crazy, smoking, and drinking. I guess I was just ignorant because I never saw it that way. The lack of money caused unhappiness and depression, but smoking nor drinking never crossed my mind.

I tell you, only God does what He does. He gives us new opportunities every day. God is taking us to another level. We heard preachers say for years, "This is your year." Why would you tell the

WHY YOU WANT TO KNOW ABOUT ME?

church, "This is your year," *every* year? If this is your year, and I am preaching that every year, and I have been in your church for many years, and I am looking for something, and I see nothing.

I am not saying that God has not done anything. It goes back to your choices and decisions. You will only see something if you are making great decisions. That may be because you have yet to put yourself in a position to see or do something. So, there are only two things: see and do.

Life is the choice you and I make. I take a physical inventory of my life every Sunday after church. First, I asked myself, what did I do from Sunday to Sunday? Then, I check with God each week on what I can do better. I can always do something better. Finally, I allow the Holy Spirit to show me what I did wrong, so I can make sure not to do those things again.

I love this weekly exercise. I also allow the Spirit to show me what I did right and how to improve. Now I want to know what not to do. I believe this happens often: we want to know what to do better, but no one asks God what *not* to do. That is more important than knowing what to do.

When God told me "No," that was one of the greatest gifts He could have ever given me. The same is true for you. Understanding the power of NO excites me! NO will take us all to a different level because He loves us so much. He saves us.

Think of buying a home. The home-buying process is an exciting time of possibilities. You will hear about escrow in two scenarios: when you close on a home and a long-term account to manage property taxes and insurance premiums for your home. Why do you think escrow is required when you buy a home? You may think of the mediator who holds your earnest money deposit on your future home or the mortgage lender who collects and holds a portion of your monthly mortgage payment to pay the taxes and insurance.

Look at it in the spiritual context. If God has something for you, you must be able to receive the blessing. Your seat at the closing table is reserved, but you must follow the guidance of your real estate professional. Every day is a step closer to closing. You do not just go to closing after you put an offer in on a home. There are inspections, repairs, closing costs, and other necessary steps to seal the deal. He uses escrow to protect us. I thank God for His protection. I know He protected me to deliver His prophetic message. I feel proud when God allows me to bless someone; however, what makes me feel better is when God trusts me enough to deliver His message. They will know about God when I finish – How God turned my life around. So, *Why do you want to know about me?* This process taught me that my journey and growth in Christ are not about me but about Him. I will leave you with this final scripture from Galatians 2:20 (NIV):

"I have been crucified with Christ, and I no longer live, but Christ lives in me. The life I now live in the body, I live by faith in the Son of God, who loved me and gave himself for me."

I know I am God's favorite, and so are you!

Acknowledgments

*Therefore, since we are surrounded
by such a great cloud of witnesses,
let us throw off everything that hinders
and the sin that so easily entangles.
And let us run with perseverance
the race marked out for us…*
Hebrews 12:1 (NIV)

I would like to extend a huge thank you to all those who supported and helped make this book a reality. Your kindness, creativity, and hard work have been invaluable in the success of this project. I am so grateful for all you have done, and I could not have done it without your prayers and support.

Grateful acknowledgment is made to Bishop Dr. Leonard Lacey, Founder, and Senior Pastor of United Faith Christian Ministry (UFCM), Stafford, VA. Bishop Lacey helped me to grow spiritually through his wisdom. He provided tough love and guidance in my business, as well as my personal growth. Bishop Lacey truly has a love for people and saving souls. He is heavily involved in Community Outreach Programs. Bishop Lacey is a great administrator, preacher, and teacher. I am glad to call him a friend.

SHERMAN HARRIS, JR

Reverend Isaac Samuels, Assistant Pastor, and Lead Choir Director, United Faith Christian Ministry (UFCM), Stafford, VA. Rev. Samuels was my spiritual confidant and sounding board. He assisted and answered many questions when I needed clarification. We had great conversations about interpreting scriptures, sermons, and the Word of God. Rev. Samuels is a great listener, preacher, and teacher. I feel comfortable talking to him; I am glad to call him a friend.

Rev. Dr. John Eaves, Pastor of the Youth Ministry, United Faith Christian Ministry (UFCM), Stafford, VA. Rev. Eaves is a great preacher and teacher. He loves the Lord and has a great passion for teaching our youth. I had the opportunity to be involved in several business ventures with him. I have watched the move of God on this young man and have seen him grow spiritually. Rev. Eaves is a great businessman and entrepreneur. I am glad to call Rev. John Eaves a friend.

Rev. Tremayne Lacey, Pastor of Education and Director of Unity Institute (TUI), United Faith Christian Ministry (UFCM), Stafford, VA. Rev. Tremayne Lacey is a great preacher and teacher. He has a way of teaching that makes you think outside the box. His unique preaching and teaching make the Word of God relatable to today's issues. Rev. Tremayne Lacey truly loves the Lord, which shows his passion for teaching. I did not think we would become friends when I first met this young man, but I am glad we did.

Last but not least, my favorite ladies:

My wife, Debbie, is an incredible asset to our team. She has provided us with support, guidance, and encouragement throughout this process. We are incredibly grateful for her dedication and willingness to go above and beyond to bring this book to life.

WHY YOU WANT TO KNOW ABOUT ME?

The late Dr. Renee Lacey, First Lady at United Faith Christian Ministry (UFCM). She was truly my cheerleader and advocate for my business. I received a myriad of referrals for my business, including their home. She ministered to me about my humbleness, not being afraid of my gift, and trusting God. Dr. Renee Lacey truly loved the Lord, and I learned to worship through her ministering through song. She advocated for non-traditional education and ensured all students' needs were met.

Deacon Angeline Black, Deacon's Ministry, United Faith Christian Ministry (UFCM), Stafford, VA. A woman who truly loves the Lord. She helped me gain different interpretations of scripture(s) and issues that needed to be biblically clear to me. We took classes together at UFCM's Unity Institute and had great discussions. We both serve as members of UFCM's Intercessory Prayer Ministry. Angeline is a great prayer warrior and has prayed for and with me numerous times.

Most importantly, I would like to thank Dr. Jacque Eaves for making this book come to fruition. She has been the project manager and spearheaded a team to oversee my book through completion. Dr. Jacque Eaves spent countless hours, days, and months to make this book possible. God told me Jacque was the one to accept this challenge, and she has done a stellar job!

My favorite ladies are beautiful inside and out; they truly love the Lord and people and have a heart of gold.

SHERMAN HARRIS, JR

Let's Stay Connected

Visit me online at www.ShermanHarrisJr.com
Submit your prayer requests and praise reports.

Iron Sharpen Iron
Men are invited to join me each
Monday at 6:00 a.m. EST
Conference Call Number:
(267) 807-9495
Code: 993895307

For Encouragement Call
540-300-2183
For a special recorded message

Follow on All Social Media Platforms
@prophetshermanharrisjr

For Bookings and Speaking Engagements
571-766-8733
info@chandragoreconsulting.com

www.ingramcontent.com/pod-product-compliance
Lightning Source LLC
Chambersburg PA
CBHW070906160426
43194CB00033B/1710